The DEAD 1704.

The Stebbins Family
in Colonial New England
1634 – 1724

The DEAD 1704.

The Stebbins Family in Colonial New England
1634 – 172

Henry R. Stebbins, Jr.

ISBN: 978-0-578-51283-9

Henry R. Stebbins, Jr.
131 Thunder Trail
Cranston, RI 02921
sailnut143@verizon.net

In Conjunction With
Husky Trail Press LLC
7 Hurlbutt Road, Unit J-10
Gales Ferry, CT 06335
info@huskytrailpress.com
www.HuskyTrailPress.com

Front Cover:
Altered photo of the mass gravesite in Old Deerfield,
Photographer - Henry R. Stebbins, Jr

Printed in the U.S.A.
All rights reserved

Notice of Liability. Every precaution has been taken in the preparation of this book and the information in this book is distributed on an "as is" basis, without warranty.

DEDICATION

To the memory of my dear sister, Andrea. She asked a number of questions in order to fulfill the requirements for a research paper, and opened my eyes with the relatively limited things she discovered. As a result, I expanded upon her work. I'm very sad over the fact that she died before she could see where I've taken my research; it was her dream.

ACKNOWLEDGMENT

I want to thank my wife, Dianne, for her patience during the production of this work; for her technical assistance in proof reading the initial drafts; for supplying the subscription to Ancestry.com; and for her love of historical stories in general.

TABLE OF CONTENTS

ILLUSTRATIONS XI
MAPS XIII
PREFACE XV
INTRODUCTION XVII
    Overview XVII
    Background XVII

Chapter 1   JUVENILE DELINQUENTS 19

Chapter 2   KING PHILIP'S WAR 23
    A Family Relationship 23
    Overview 23
    The Indian's Perspective 25
    Bloody Brook 31
    Turner's Falls Massacre 39
    Return to Deerfield 42

Chapter 3   THE STRANGE DEATH OF JOHN STEBBINS, SENIOR 45

Chapter 4   PERMANENT SETTLEMENT 47

Chapter 5   KING WILLIAM'S WAR 53

Chapter 6   THE SARAH SMITH AFFAIR 57

Chapter 7   QUEEN ANNE'S WAR: 59
    The War of the Spanish Succession 59
    French/Indian Motives 61
    Initial Preparations 65
    Preliminary Action 69
    Deerfield's Cry for Support 70

	Stebbins Connection with the Frenchmen and Illegal Fur-trade	79
	French/Indian Preparations	84
Chapter 8	DEERFIELD: Raid or Massacre?	87
Chapter 9	ADDITIONAL NOTES ON THE BATTLE	103
	Watchman Controversy	103
	Fatal Wounding of the Frenchman	104
	Sheldon House's Door	105
	Benoni Stebbins House	106
Chapter 10	FORCE MARCHED INTO CAPTIVITY	109
	Considerations	109
	Route of the Captives	111
	Care of the Captives	112
Chapter 11	POST BATTLE FALLOUT	115
	Compensation for Scalps, Plunder and Losses	115
	Stebbins-Related Aftermath	118
	Deerfield as a Military Post	118
Chapter 12	REDEMPTION OF CAPTIVES	125
	Sheldon's First Expedition to Canada	125
	Sheldon's Second Expedition to Canada	130
	Sheldon's Third Expedition to Canada	134
Chapter 13	THE CLOSE OF QUEEN ANNE'S WAR	137
	1705	137
	1706	137
	1707	138
	1708	140
	1709	142
	1710	143
	1711	145
	1712	145

Chapter 14 THE AFTERMATH OF QUEEN ANNE'S WAR 151
    Fate of the John Stebbins Jr's Family 151
    Redeemed 153
        John Stebbins, Jr.: 153
        Dorothy Stebbins: 154
        Samuel: 154
        John Stebbins [III]: 154
        Aaron Denio [De Noyon]: 155
    Unredeemed 156
        Joseph Stebbins: 156
        Ebenezer Stebbins: 156
        Abigail De Noyon [Marguerite Denio]: 157
        Thankful Stebbins: 160
        Eunice Williams: 161

Chapter 15 SUBSEQUENT DEERFIELD WARS 163
    Father Rasle's War or Drummer's War (1722-1724) 163
    French and Indian War or the Old French War (1754-1763) 165

    APPENDIX A 168
    APPENDIX B 170
    APPENDIX C 172

    ENDNOTES 183
    BIBLIOGRAPHY 205
    INDEX 209

    AUTHOR'S BIOGRAPHY 215

ILLUSTRATIONS

Rowland Stebbins 18
Milewski Homestead 22
King Philip 24
Bloody Brook Attack 35
Bloody Brook Monument 37
Reverend John Williams 49
Queen Mary 53
King William III 53
Queen Anne 59
King Louis XIV 60
Abenaki Clothing 63
Phillipe de Rigand de Vaudreuil 64
Jean Baptiste Hertel de Rouville 64
Governor Joseph Dudley 65
Colonel Peter Schuyler 69
Canadian Snowshoe Ranger 80
Indian Head Breaker 92
John Sheldon's House 93
Macqua Chief 98
John Sheldon's House Door 106
'Death of Father Sebastian Rasle' 164
George Washington 165

MAPS

Map 1: Algonquian Tribes of New England 27
Map 2: Connecticut River Valley 41
Map 3: The Northeast 68
Map 4: Early Deerfield 77
Map 5: Palisade 90
Map 6: Captive's Route 113
Map 7: Boucherville 1673 148

PREFACE

When we are in our youth many of us do not appreciate the circumstances of our history. Instead of inquiring about our ancestry, we just go about our everyday existence. Had we questioned our older living relatives; we would be aware of a family history that would disappear otherwise. I continued the research, occasionally asking my Mother questions when I needed to overcome any roadblocks. I didn't ask enough questions. There are still missing facts that she or her sister could have answered. Now both are dead – missed opportunities and the information is lost forever.

What a wealth of information is out there, in spite of libraries that burned down and government files that were destroyed because of the ravages of time. Having spent hundreds of hours with the intriguing details of piecing together the puzzle of my ancestry, I don't want it to go for naught. As a result, I'm publishing the results of my quest in every way that I can, so that my children, grandchildren, etc. will not have to work to duplicate the rich tapestry of our heritage. I had the fortune of being born into a family with an adventuresome, exciting history that has become the legacy of the Stebbins family. In addition, I am now married to a woman, Dianne, with an equally colorful family history.

While the main thrust of my effort was the compilation of documented historical family information, there remains a bias in that information. Most of my sources were by English authors and reflected the perspective of their times. For King Phillips War, with the aid of Russell Bourne's book *The Red King's Rebellion Racial Politics in New England 1675-1678,* I have tried to balance some of that bias by including some perspective from the native point of view.

INTRODUCTION

Overview

Two brothers in the Stebbins family find themselves in a clash of racial, religious, and political events in early Colonial New England.

Background

The history of the first generations of Stebbins in Colonial New England was greatly shaped by the wars of that period: King Phillips War, King Williams War, and Queen Anne's War. It was, however, Queen Anne's War, that determined the destiny of my branch of the Stebbins ancestors. It is a story of captives, redeemed and un-redeemed, that focused on a small frontier town called Deerfield.

Deerfield Massachusetts, built on a fertile plain at the confluence of the Deerfield and Connecticut Rivers, began as an earlier settlement named Pocumtuck; a settlement that had been abandoned during King Phillips War. Two brothers, John Stebbins Jr., my great(x6) grandfather, and Benoni Stebbins, were typical examples of the raw pioneer spirit that settled New England. Their father, John Stebbins Sr., bought land in Pocumtuck through the auspices of a friend, John Pynchon of Springfield. By a vote, on August 26, 1668, "Left Fisher had leave to sell to John Stebbins [Sr] of Northampton, his rights at Pocumtuck, or a part of them."[1]

John Stebbins Sr., was the son of Rowland Stebbins, who arrived in Boston in 1634 aboard the *Francis* with his wife and 4 children. He moved to Northampton and had ultimately died there. He gave the Deerfield lots to his sons to be settled and farmed. Thus, the stage was set for the wars that involved the lives of Benoni and

John Jr., including Queen Anne's War, just one of the Colonial wars that resulted from wars fought in Europe.

Rowland Stebbins
1592-1671
(Ancestry.com)

Chapter 1

JUVENILE DELINQUENTS

The following is taken from the record of John Pynchon, Justice of the Peace, Springfield Massachusetts:

> May 2. 1655. John Stebbixs [Jr.] being taken notice for misbehaving himself toward his aged ffather calling him 'old foole', uttering those unseemly words toward him. was this daj aforesaid examined thereof, the matter beinge not ripe for a fynall issue the said John Stebbixs did before the commissioners bynd himself in the sume of fforty pounds to appear before authority here established to make answer for the said misbehaving himself to his ffather when he shall be thereunto required. This matter beinge further considered there was not found full proof of such evil carriage, whereof he was released and discharged of his bond above mentioned.[1]

When he was twelve years old, Benoni Stebbins and other Northampton lads, found themselves in Court. A friendly Indian, Juauguelatt, entertained them with romantic stories of the jolly camp life of the French up the river, of the gay trappings of the officers, of the merry dances with pretty maidens, and convinced them to run away to the French in Canada.[2]

Failing in their endeavor, they found themselves in Court on the morning of the 24th of September, 1667, the day the Court began its fall session. A constable armed with a long, black staff tipped with brass, having three youths in charge, forces his way through the crowd. They have been sent by the commissioners at Northampton, to be tried and sentenced at Springfield.[3] The record tells the story:

Henry R. Stebbins Jr.

September 24, 1667. Att the County Court holden att Springfield, Capt. John Pynchon one of the Honored Assistants of this Colony presiding, "James Bennett, Godfrey Nims and Benoni Stebbins, young lads of Northampton being by Northampton Commissioners bound over to this Court to answere for diverse crimes and misdeeds committed by them, were brought to this court by ye constable of y^t town, wch 3 lads are accufed by Robert Bartlett, for that they gott into his house two Sabbath days, when all the family were at Publike Meeting, on ye first of which tymes, they viz Nims and Stebbins did ransack about the house, and took away out of diverse places of the house viz, 24 shillings in silver and 7 sh. in Wampum, with intention to run away to the ffrench, all wch is by them confessed; wch wickedness of theirs hath allso been accompanied with frequent lying to excuse and justify themselves especially on Nims his part, who it seems hath been a ringleader in the villanyes; ffor all which there crimes and misdemeads this corte doth judge y^t the said 3 lads shall be well whipt on their naked bodies, viz Nims and Bennett with 25 lashes apeece and Benoni Stebbyngs with 11 lashes; and the said Nims and Stebbins are to pay Robert Bartlett the sum of 4 pounds being accounted treble damage, according to the law for what goods he hath lost by their means. Allso those persons that have received any money of any of the said lads, are to restore it to the s^d Robert Bartlett. But their being made to the Corte and earneft pitition & request by Ralph Hutchinson, father-in-law to ye said Bennett, and diverse other considerable persons, that the said Bennett's corporall punishment might be released, by reason of his mother's weaknese, who it seemed may suffer much inconvenience whereby, that punishment was remitted upon his father in law his engaging to this corte, to pay ffive pounds to ye County, as a fyne for the said Bennetts offense; which 5 pounds is to be paid to ye County Treasurer for ye use of Sd County. Also John Stebbins Junior, being much suspected to have some hand in their plotting to run away,

> this Corte doth order ye commissioners of Northampton to call him before y^m, & to examine him about that, or any other thing wherein he is supposed to be guilty with ye said lads and to act therein according to their discretion attending law. Also, they are to call the Indian called Onequelat, who had a hand with y^m in their plott, and to deale with him according as they fynd."[4]

The three, thoroughly scared boys were sent back next day to Northampton. There, let us hope little Benoni was taken from the grasp of the law, and put into his father's hands for chastisement. Bennett's fine was paid by his stepfather. As for Godfrey Nims he paid the penalty of his misdeeds at the whipping post in front of the meeting-house. Alas for Godfrey! He lived in an age when a spade was called a spade. Lying was lying in the good old colony days. Nobody thought of applying to the wild boy the soft impeachment of being an imaginative youth.[5]

Later, in 1674, he [John Stebbins Jr.] would be embroiled in another case, as five people accused him of 'lascivious carriage.'[6]

Milewski Homestead
with Bloody Brook in the background.
H. Stebbins, 2000

Chapter 2

KING PHILIP'S WAR

A Family Relationship

The war of 1675-6 is often known as King Philip's War, though no strong evidence has him intimately participating in all the skirmishes attributed to him.

The Stebbins were embroiled in the conflicts of early Puritan New England. My great(x6) grandfather, John Stebbins Jr., was one of four known survivors of the massacre at Bloody Brook in 1675, at a location now known as South Deerfield MA. In one of those strange coincidences that often occur, my maternal grandparents emigrated from Poland and eventually lived on a farm a short distance from the Bloody Brook site. Their son, Kazimierz A. Milewski, unearthed hundreds of arrowheads while plowing the fields, perhaps some from the battle itself. My mother married into the same branch of the Stebbins family that are direct descendants of John; thus, completing the historical connection.

Overview

When King Philip's war spread to western Massachusetts, soldiers were sent from the eastern part of the Massachusetts Bay Province to defend the river towns. The problem of feeding these troops became so crucial that on September 18, 1675, Capt. Lathrop and his company from Essex were dispatched to Deerfield to escort a wagon train of wheat to the headquarters at Hadley. The company set out for Hadley with 17 Deerfield teamsters and ox-carts, but when they came to the small stream along the way, they dropped their weapons and began to eat wild grapes growing on nearby vines. Suddenly and without warning, a band of 1000 Indians rose up from ambush and fell upon the unsuspecting English. Sixty-four teamsters and soldiers were slain in this encounter which had been ever since known as the Bloody Brook Massacre. The famous Brook still flows through South Deerfield, but happily its waters no longer run red even though it retains its reminiscent name. Following this disaster, Deerfield was abandoned, and once more Indians occupy the settlement.[1]

Bloody Brook took place in the greater context of King Philip's war. Historian Michael Tougias describes the war as follows:

> The bloodiest war in America's history, on a per capita basis, took place in New England in 1675. At the center of this cataclysm was one man, Metacom, leader of the Pokanokets, a tribe within the Wampanoag Indian Federation. At an early age, when relations between the natives and settlers were less stressed, Metacom was given the nickname of King Philip by the English, because of his haughty mannerisms. One of the many ironies of this conflict is that Philip was the son of Massasoit -- the same Massasoit who had helped the Plymouth Pilgrims survive their first winter in the New World. A father's kindness would become a son's curse. In the 55-year span between the arrival of the Mayflower and the outbreak of King Philip's War, the English had prospered, multiplied and expanded their settlements while the natives were in a slow state of decline from diseases introduced by the Europeans and loss of tribal lands to the whites. By 1675, with the stage now fully set for conflict, Philip stepped forward to make a stand. In a prophetic moment he warned the whites of his intentions, saying "I am determined not to live until I have no country." The war actually began after Wampanoag braves killed some English owned cattle near their

King Philip
(Shultz & Tougias)

tribal headquarters in what is now Bristol, Rhode Island. English livestock was always a source of friction as cattle repeatedly trampled Indian corn. A farmer then retaliated by killing an Indian, setting in motion a native uprising that would eventually threaten to wipe Massachusetts Bay and Plymouth Bay Colonies out of existence. The Nipmuck Indians, who lived in what is now central Massachusetts, joined forces with Philip's Wampanoags. Together they presented a very formidable force. Next the Nipmuck and Wampanoag warriors turned their attention to the settlements along the Connecticut River Valley. The fertile valley along the Connecticut River produced thousands of bushels of grain each year and was known as the breadbasket of New England. English farms were scattered throughout the region. The natives knew the population was sparse there compared to the Boston area. In autumn of 1675, the Nipmucks and Wampanoags were joined on the warpath by tribes that lived along the Connecticut River including the Pocumtucks (residing along the northern part of the river), Squakheags (residing in present day Northfield) and the Norwottocks (greater Hadley). They concentrated their attacks on the area known as Pioneer Valley and attacked the town of Deerfield (known to natives as Pemawachuatuck "at the twisted mountain") causing the town to be abandoned by the English.[2]

The Indian's Perspective

The face of New England in the 1670's was like a figure by Picasso, wracked by change and disruption. First and foremost: its native peoples had been so destroyed by European diseases that in southern New England not twenty thousand remained of Algonquian-speaking peoples who had once numbered three or four times that number, "the flower and strength" having been killed by European microbes against which the natives had no defense. By contrast, there were some fifty thousand English colonists, growing in number and in power.[3]

Unlike the more relaxed attitude that the French up north had for the natives, the Puritans had a strict code of conduct that they enforced – even on their own people. In spite of that strict moral code, the bi-racial society in New England lasted for over 50 years with surprisingly few problems.

Russell Bourne felt that:

> The great diplomats of the first two generations of red-white contact were succeeded by a new generation of less accommodating, more bitter personages, of whom Metacom, or Philip, was one and Major Josiah Winslow was another. The political solutions that had been worked out by such geniuses as Roger Williams in Rhode Island and Passaconaway in Massachusetts and New Hampshire gave way to feuds, flare-ups, and brutal repressions. It's for this reason that I came to see the entire scene in terms of a political implosion, a collapse of creative political solutions.[4]

Bourne summarizes the works of various authors in terms their reason for the conflict between the races:

> Even a modern explanation in Francis Jennings work, *The Invasion of America,* suggests the Puritans were following an Old Testament philosophy 'that they should subdue the earth and have dominion over everything that moves on earth.' [This sounds like a type of "manifest destiny" to me.] In addition, his theory is that the Puritans and their cohorts the Pilgrims carefully planned and executed two massive aggressions against New England's Algonquians: the Pequot War of 1636-1637 and King Phillips War. Jennings further believes these were both 'outright land grabs, illegal and unjustifiable usurpations of native territories by
>
> the English would-be estate owners.'[5]
>
> Hubbard described Massachusetts Bay as "the Israel of God" on the march in the New World; whatever the

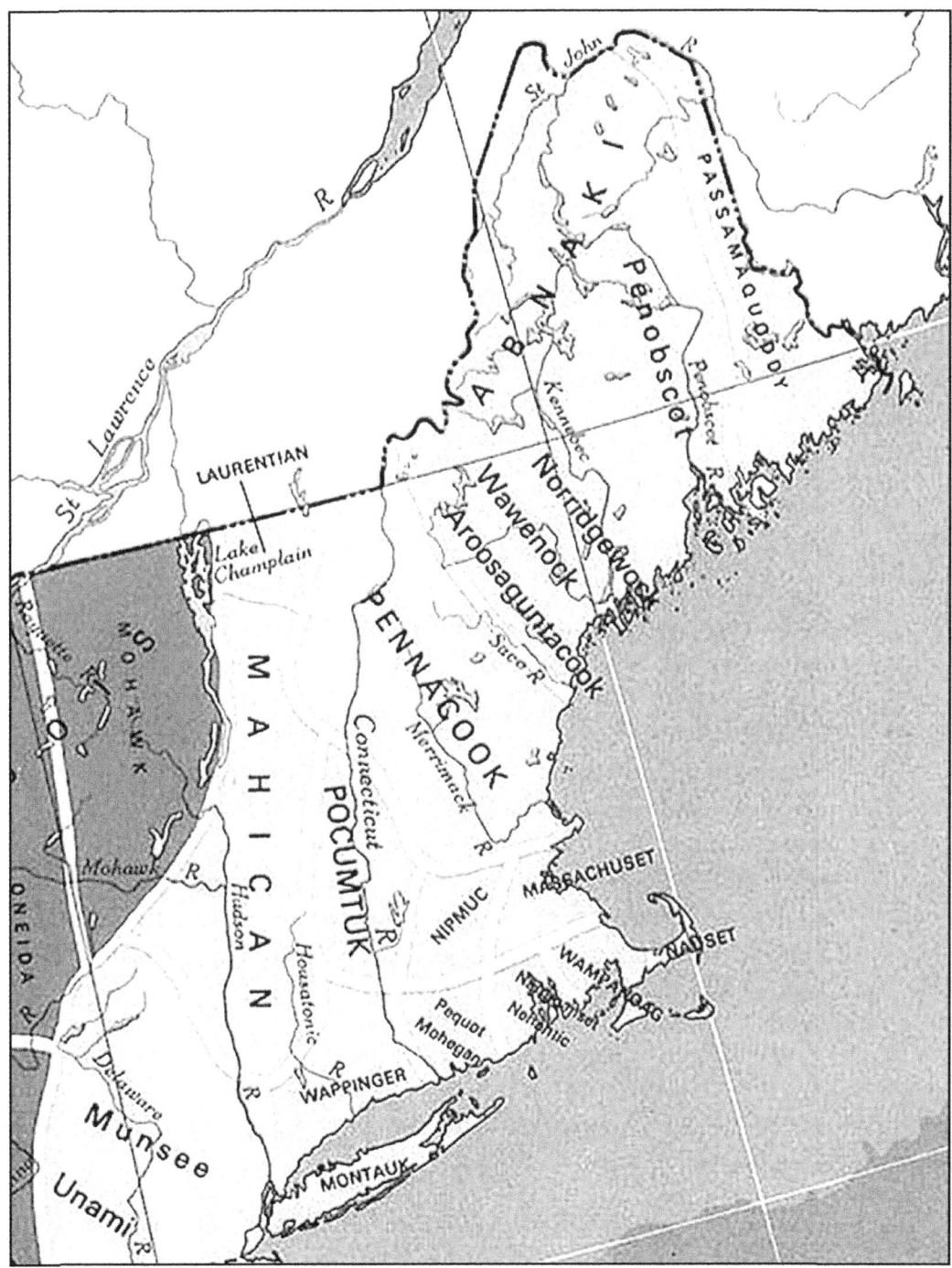

Map 1: Algonquian Tribes of New England
https://upload.wikimedia.org/wikipedia/commons/a/aa/Early_Localization_Native_Americans_USA.jpg

morally right], carried out in his name by his triumphant warriors. There is but one side in his narrative, the cause of armored righteousness.[6]

In general, revisionists find the Puritans perverse and the Algonquians in perfect harmony with nature. The natives 'washed themselves more than the English, needed no prisons or magistrates because there was no crime among them, and fought in a truly less savage way (indulging in neither torture nor rapes, both of which were common features in European soldiery)'.[7] "The Pilgrims have 'stringent laws and ordinances upon the subject of fornication and adultery, which laws they maintain and enforce very "strictly indeed", even among the tribes that live amongst them."[8]

Behind all this, is the fact that "the face of New England in the 1670's was like a figure by Picasso, wracked by change and disruption. First and foremost: its native peoples had been so destroyed by European diseases that in southern New England not twenty thousand remained of Algonquian-speaking peoples who had once numbered three or four times that number, "the flower and strength" having been killed by European microbes against which the natives had no defense. By contrast, there were some fifty thousand English colonists, growing in number and in power."[9] As a result, population pressure was rapidly favoring the settlers.

Another factor in the slow march toward the disaster called King Philips War was the erosion of the economic opportunities that the natives suffered. Bourne outlines his argument as follows:

> Commercial life in this part of America had the gone on to become a fundamental aspect of existence. The issue for Phillip and his people was not whether to be included in the evolution of seventeenth-century commercialism,

but what to do if their status as trading partners was ever undermined by a lack of demand for their basic products. To become trading partners in northern New England, the Algonquian residents of those beaver-rich woodlands needed to alter their traditional ways very little. But the *southern* Algonquians, having determined that the best course for them was to turn to the production of wampum, made radical shifts in how they lived and how the labor of men and woman was directed.[10]

Increasingly, the lives of the natives revolved more and more around the trading post – a seemingly natural development within such a commercial society.[11] There were, of course, negative aspects within this world of traders and the fur and wampum producers; the insidiousness of alcohol; and the inequalities of the English justice system. Furthermore, the native was pushed constantly out of his value systems and into the English modes.[12]

William Cronon described in his book *Changes in the Land: Indians, Colonists, and the Ecology of New England* that the "demand for wampum fell, and the Indians on the south coast suddenly found themselves isolated from markets on which they had come to rely. Indians for whom pelts had been their main access to trade had comparable experiences when their fur supplies gave out. These changes contributed to the conflicts leading up to King Philips War.[13]

Yet many of the Connecticut valley farmers must have also nursed the hope *** that the natives who worked in *their* fields, helped grind *their* corn and build *their* houses were far too thoroughly cowed to attempt any insurrection. The time of equality between settlers and natives had obviously passed with the phasing out of wampum, but was there now a convenient and well-established master-servant relationship? Or would that relationship prove so corruptive as to wreck the frontier society John Pynchon worked to advance? Deerfield would be the scene of the first military activity of King Philips War in the valley, gives one small answer to that large question.[14]

Up and down the valley there was an unhealthy pattern of unequal and discriminatory relations between the thriving settlers and the displaced natives. Now that they could no longer barter venison or beaver for the needed and desired English goods, the women tried to sell baskets or birch brooms, the men to work at menial agriculture tasks they despised. In the words of a perceptive nineteenth-century writer, the natives 'saw themselves sinking in degradation and subservience before the rising power of their white neighbors.' Or in the cruelly apt phrase of nationalist historian George Bancroft, they came to depend on and even love 'the crums from the white man's table.'[15]

In the end, Bourne said result was:

> Successive generations of American sages have sought to explain King Phillip's War to readers of their own times. First the struggle was portrayed as a classic and necessary victory for the nation yet-to-be-born. Then repressed truths gradually surfaced, such as that the rebellion had nearly succeeded: more than half of New England's towns were attacked; with refugees crowding Boston and the few safe coastal towns, the English were on the point of being driven into the sea, the Puritan theocracy discredited as weak and inept.[16]

> Though the basic material to be mined for these discoveries is severely limited, the writers have struggled to work over that material again and again and to find a root cause that will correspond to contemporary beliefs about humankind.[17]

The Dead 1704

Bloody Brook

By 1667 the land had been officially acquired: a sachem by the name of Chauk had been found to sign the deed with his mark, on behalf of all Pocumtucks. By 1669 the first purchaser of a land plot, a farmer named Samuel Hinsdale, was plowing his land. And by 1670 the main street and subsidiary ways had been laid out. And by 1673, after independence was won from Dedham, the first church was established. With the meetinghouse framed and roofed, Samuel Mather was called in 1675 to be the first minister. There were more than twenty families in the village to greet him when he rode up Main Street. *** At the heart of the village was a fenced-in common; livestock was allowed to forage on the hillsides during the grazing season, and the natives did not seem to mind.[18]

As for the remaining Pocumtucks and other regional Algonquians, it appeared that they made adequate provision for themselves in the initial land deeds. The Pocumtucks had retained for themselves the rights to hunt, fish, and gather wild fruits and nuts even on land staked out by the settlers. *** Although the deeds seemed fair, they concealed a heavy-handed paternalism. The natives were imagined to be frozen in their own, primitive economy. Although they would pick up whatever they could forage and work for the settlers when needed, playing a marginal role at the fringe of this prosperous, new-agricultural community with its improved iron tools and strong marketing ties to the commercial world beyond, they would own no part of it. Psychologically or physically.[19]

With Hadley named headquarters for the three troops sent by Massachusetts Bay to secure this vital region in early summer 1675, settler-native relations grew even tenser. John Pynchon urged everyone around him not to overreact to the news from distant Swansea, but few listened. He protested his unfitness for any military position but had to agree when the title of commander in chief was forced upon him.[20]

Then in August came the report of the Brookfield siege. The military at Hadley immediately demanded that the neighboring, "threatening" Norwottocks surrender their weapons – which would among other things, prevent them from hunting and supporting themselves. When, briefly, after the Norwottocks came up with the ingenious idea of joining the soldiers in a search for the westward-wandering Quaboags (the presumed attackers of Brookfield), the weapons were returned to them. But it seemed to the three commanders at Hadley – Captains Watts, Lothrop, and Beers - that the Norwottocks had been less than enthusiastic in their search; neither any Quaboags nor any other hostile Nipmucks had been found. Indeed, there were signs that the Norwottocks were fortifying their village on the west bank of the Connecticut, all too close to Hatfield, turning it into a strongpoint for their own warriors and for other River Indians. So the commanders decided to get the weapons back.[21]

A swift-footed native informer carried the news of the English commander's decision to the Norwottocks camp, causing the people to gather around the council fire to debate their possible options. *** An elderly Norwottock stood up to suggest that, if patience were applied, surely the current contentions would pass away and the former times of mutually advantageous harmony would return. *** Younger braves demanded action against the English. When the elderly sachem stood up again, he was killed with a blow from a young brave's tomahawk.[22]

Captains Lothrop and Beers, on finding the native fortress evacuated, set off in pursuit of the Norwottocks with a force of one hundred. But native tactics proved a match for English might. As the soldiers hurried along the trail, climbing the ridge (Sugarloaf Mountain), that rises between South Deerfield and the river they fell into a trap carefully prepared by the Norwottocks' rear guard. In the sharp action that followed, nine of the English soldiers were slain, and the bulk Norwottocks of the fleeing natives were able to reach the Pocumtuck's village.[23]

The valley frontier burst into flames: Deerfield was struck again and Northfield was subjected to a large-scale attack in which eight settlers were killed and wide damage done to farms and crops. When a relief expedition of thirty-six troopers and teamsters under Captain Beers rolled up the valley to Northfield, it was virtually wiped out at a ford south of the town. The siege that followed, staged by Squakheags plus other allies, was finally broken by Connecticut's Robert Treat and his downriver colonials.[24] In the distressed and fearful mood of the day, hatred Became a racial matter.[25]

Again, at Deerfield, shortly after the momentous decision was made by the military to withdraw all settlers from Northfield, the event took place over the course of several days and opened on September 12, a Sunday, when watchful Pocumtucks fell upon worshipers returning along Main Street to the Stockwell garrison from Deerfield's meetinghouse. As settlers swiftly took cover, only one man was killed, but two houses were burned and a number of horses and wagonloads of beef were taken. A force of English soldiers, dispatched to round up the local raiders, could find no one as they combed the nearby hills.[26]

The Bay's strategy, if it can be called that, was simple: while Captain Lothrop was ordered to Deerfield to protect the harvest from local attackers, Moseley and his gang would seek out mightier enemies, the Nipmucks, wherever they may be.[27]

The massacre at Bloody Brook, September 18th 1675, was one of those attacks. The following modern account by Richard Melvoin details the attack:

> In stacks in the Pocumtuck meadows stood over three thousand bushels of corn. With a besieged valley to feed, the food's value was obvious. With a share of the grain belonging to none other than Pocumtuck entrepreneur, valley merchant, and military commander John Pynchon, desire to salvage the grain may have gained official sanction. Perhaps most important, reports were trickling in that, in this summer of war, food supplies were dwindling. As the corn stood in Pocumtuck's fields, the General Court was less than a month from declaring the 'great danger of a famine'. Captain Thomas Lathrop took his company up to the town and, aided by the remaining townsmen, loaded the grain onto carts. On a Saturday morning, September 18, while Captain Mosely and his Pocumtuck garrison sent out scouts, Lathrop and about fifty soldiers, plus fifteen 'teamsters' – Pocumtuck men recruited to help drive the caravan – headed south.[28]

As Deerfield's chronicler George Sheldon tells the story:

> Capt. Lothrop, 'with his choice company of young men, the very flower of the County of Essex' followed by a slowly moving train of carts, marched proudly down the old Town Street, two miles across South Meadows, up Bars Long Hill, to the heavily wooded plain stretching away to Hatfield meadows. Southward along the narrow Pocumtuck path, through the primeval woods, moved Lothrop and his men – brave, fearless, foolish. Confident in their numbers, scorning danger, not even a vanguard or a flanker was thrown out.

Meanwhile the whole hostile force was lying like serpents in the way; but unlike the more chivalric of these reptiles their fangs will be felt before a warning is given. The probable leaders were Mattamuck, Sagamore Sam, Matoonas and One-Eyed John, of the Nipmucks; Anawan, Penchason, and Tatason, of the Wampanoags, and Sangumachu of the remnant of the Pocumtucks. There is no evidence that Philip was present, and the probabilities are against it.

Keen eyes had seen the preparation for Lothrop's march; swift feet had carried the news to the chieftains below, who at this moment were giving their last orders to their warriors lying in ambush at Bloody Brook, into which Lothrop was marching in fatal security. From the top of Long Hill, the path lay through the dense forest for a mile and a half, when it approached on the left a narrow, swampy thicket, trending southward, through which crept sluggishly a nameless brook. Skirting this swamp another mile, a point was reached where it narrowed and turned to the right. Here the path crossed it diagonally, leaving the marsh on the right.

The soldiers crossed the brook and halted, while the teams should slowly drag their heavy loads through the mire; 'many of them' says Mather 'having been so foolish and secure to put their arms in the carts and step aside to gather grapes, which proved dear and deadly grapes to them.' Meanwhile the silent morass on either flank was covered with grim warriors prone upon the ground, their tawny bodies indistinguishable from the slime in which they crawled, or their scarlet plumes and crimson paint from the glowing tints of the dying year on leaf and vine. Eagerly but breathless and still, they waited the signal. The critical moment had come. The fierce war-whoop rang in the ears of the astonished English.[29]

Russell Bourne had some interesting details at this point:

The Dead 1704

Captain Lothrop should have suspected what lay ahead when his wagons encountered a large number of trees that had been felled across the southward track at Muddy Brook. The train of carts halted, those in the rear piling up on those in front. Amid the shouting and confusion, the first musket shots were heard. It was an ambush.[30]

Sheldon continues:

> The men of Pocumtuck sank, the Flower of Essex withered before it, and the nameless stream was baptized in blood. Over sixty men lay dead on what one contemporary called 'that most fatal day, the saddest that ever befel New-England.' It was, indeed, a disaster – as bad as any the English suffered in the entire war.[31]

Bloody Brook Attack
(Shultz & Tougias 170)

C. Alice Baker adds:

> Many of the soldiers had stacked or laid down their guns, and, in conscious security, were regaling themselves upon the delicious grapes which were found there in great abundance, growing upon the vines which were entwined

around the trees at that place. In a moment the guns of the whole body of Indians, who were lying in wait for their victims, poured destruction upon their ranks, accompanied by the terrific yells of the savage war-whoop. Capt. Lathrop and the greater part of his soldiers fell on the first attack. Those who remained fought with the ferocity of tigers; but what avail were skill and bravery against such a disparity of numbers? [32]

George Sheldon continues:

> Moseley, who with about sixty men had gone out from Deerfield to range the woods in another direction, 'hearing the reports that the guns gave of this battel, came up with a handful of men too late.' He arrived on the scene about 10 o'clock in the morning and found the savages plundering the carts and stripping the dead. They had ripped open the bags of grain and the feather beds, and scattered the contents in the bloody mire.[33]

Russell Bourne adds:

> But suddenly they were caught themselves in a rain of bullets from the surrounding woods; Moseley's seventy troopers, alerted by the sounds of battle, now charged down from the hills. Muttawmp's men successfully fought off the counterattack, however, killing a number of the troopers.[34]

Sheldon finishes with:

> This disorganized mass was quickly driven from their prey. Among the slain lay Robert Dutch of Ipswich, who, says Hubbard his pastor, had been 'sorely wounded by a Bullet that rased his skull, and then mauled by the Indian Hatchets, and left for dead by the Savages, and stript by them of all but his skin, yet when Moseley came near, he came towards the English to their no small amazement.'

The Dead 1704

The natives recognized Moseley and were said to have taunted him: 'Come, Moseley, come! You seek Indians, you want Indians? Here is Indians enough for you!'[35]

In his account, Melvoin continues:

> That night Mosely led his troops back to the Pocumtuck garrison. When he awoke that next Sabbath morning, he rode his forces back to the site of the disaster so that they could bury the dead – only to find Indians there 'stripping the slain'. Driving away the enemy, Mosely's men carried out their gruesome task, laying the bodies in a common grave at the site [see photos].

Bloody Brook Monument
H. StebbinS, 2000

Bloody Brook Monument
H. StebbinS, 2000

Returning to Pocumtuck, Mosely's soldiers faced another sickening scene. A detachment of the victorious Indians appeared across the river from the town, insolently 'hanging up the garments of the English' slain at Bloody Brook. Even more insulting for the soldiers, some of the Indians taunted the survivors in good English. They were among John Eliot's former 'praying Indians,' his English-speaking Christian converts. Still other Indians passed by the remaining garrison house in town. With only twenty-seven soldiers left, though, Mosely dared not attack.[36]

John Jr. [Stebbins] apparently served under Lathrop as a soldier.[37] Additional evidence of ancestor John Jr.'s involvement in the battle can be found in an old account by George Sheldon in 1895:

John Stebbins of Deerfield, ancestor of all the tribe here, is the only man who is known to have escaped*, un-hurt.[38]

*The evidence of his escape is found in the following petition from the Massachusetts Archives, Vol. 69, p.208:

To the much Honoured counsel now sitting in Boston, the Humble petition of John Stebbens (of muddy River), Most Humbly sheweth, your pore petitioner, hath bene a souldier, in the service of the countrey (about a year & halfe) & was under the comand of captain Lathrope & with him when he and his company were destroyed, & under the the comand of captain Moseley the Greatest part of the time he was out, I was never forced or pressed into the service, but volenttarily gave my selfe frely to the wars of the Lord, & my country- and now of late your petitioner, hath followed in these parts his caling o A carpenter, sometimes in one towne, & sometimes in another, about 5 months I have wrought in cambridg vilage, & after my work there was finished, & removed to muddy River to doe worke there promised, the constable of the villiage, by order of the militia, came and pressed me for a garison souldier for Hadley, I went not out of the Viliage to avoid the prese, for I heard nothing of the prese, but my worke there was finished, and my selfe removed more a weke before, as may be made appear, your pore petitioner hath bene warned to appear before the committee of militia, at the viliage, for not attending that service, & by them assigned to pay fower pounds where vpon your pore petitioner, doth look upon himselfe much wronged & put to much trouble by being illegally pressed by the constable of another towne, & it hath bene the loss of much time & greatly to the damage of your petitioner-my humble request therefore to your honours is, thay you would be pleased to put an issue to the mater, or that you would be pleased to appoint a time for the hereing of the case, and that parsons concerned may have notice thereof. I cast my selfe downe at your Honours foot, and shall quietly sit downe satisfied with your Honours determination, & granting the request of your pore petitioner, he shall be farther engaged in your service, & shall not cease to pray for your Honours hapiness.

July 4th 1678 the Council on hearing of this Case declare that they judge it meet to discharge the said Stebbins from ye said fine & his surety also.

The second day after the massacre, John Stebbins Jr. enlisted under the gallant Captain Samuel Moseley, and probably served with him through King Philip's War. After remaining a few years in the vicinity of Boston, he went to Deerfield at the permanent settlement, and resided on lot number thirty-five.[39]

Turner's Falls Massacre

John's brother Benoni Stebbins evened the score for Bloody Brook by participating in the Turners Falls Massacre during the following Spring. Michael Tougias closes his article[40] with the following description of that attack:

> Captain Turner (for whom Turner's Falls is named) and Captain Holyoke (for whom the city of Holyoke is named) launched a surprise raid in May on the Indian camp at the northern end of the Connecticut River. An English boy who had escaped captivity from the Indians told the cap-

tains the exact location of the camp (at the great falls where the natives could spear fish). The soldiers immediately marched. Surprising the Indians at dawn, they slaughtered scores of natives as they fled their wigwams. Others tried to swim across the Connecticut River to escape the soldiers' muskets but drowned as the swift spring current swept them over the falls.

Warriors from surrounding areas launched a counterattack, killing Turner as his men fled back to the safety of Hadley. But the damage had been done. This major war camp of the Wampanoags and Nipmucks had been wiped out. As a result, the Indian alliance soon collapsed. The few Native Americans who survived either fled north or went on fighting in a lost cause. Philip, with only a few warriors left, made his way back to his tribal headquarters near Swansea at Mount Hope, where the war had started. Benjamin Church, using friendly Indians as scouts, tracked him throughout the summer while Philip made hit and run attacks on isolated farms in the region. But Church eventually caught up with him. An Indian who was guiding Church fired his musket and sent a musket ball through Philip's heart. The death of Philip effectively ended Native American resistance in New England. But true to his word Philip had gone down fighting "determined not to live until I have no country."

Benoni Stebbins reached his 20's unbowed and still adventuresome. Though he fought in King Philip's war, he was also among a group of men who were prosecuted and fined for wearing their hair too long in 1676.[41]

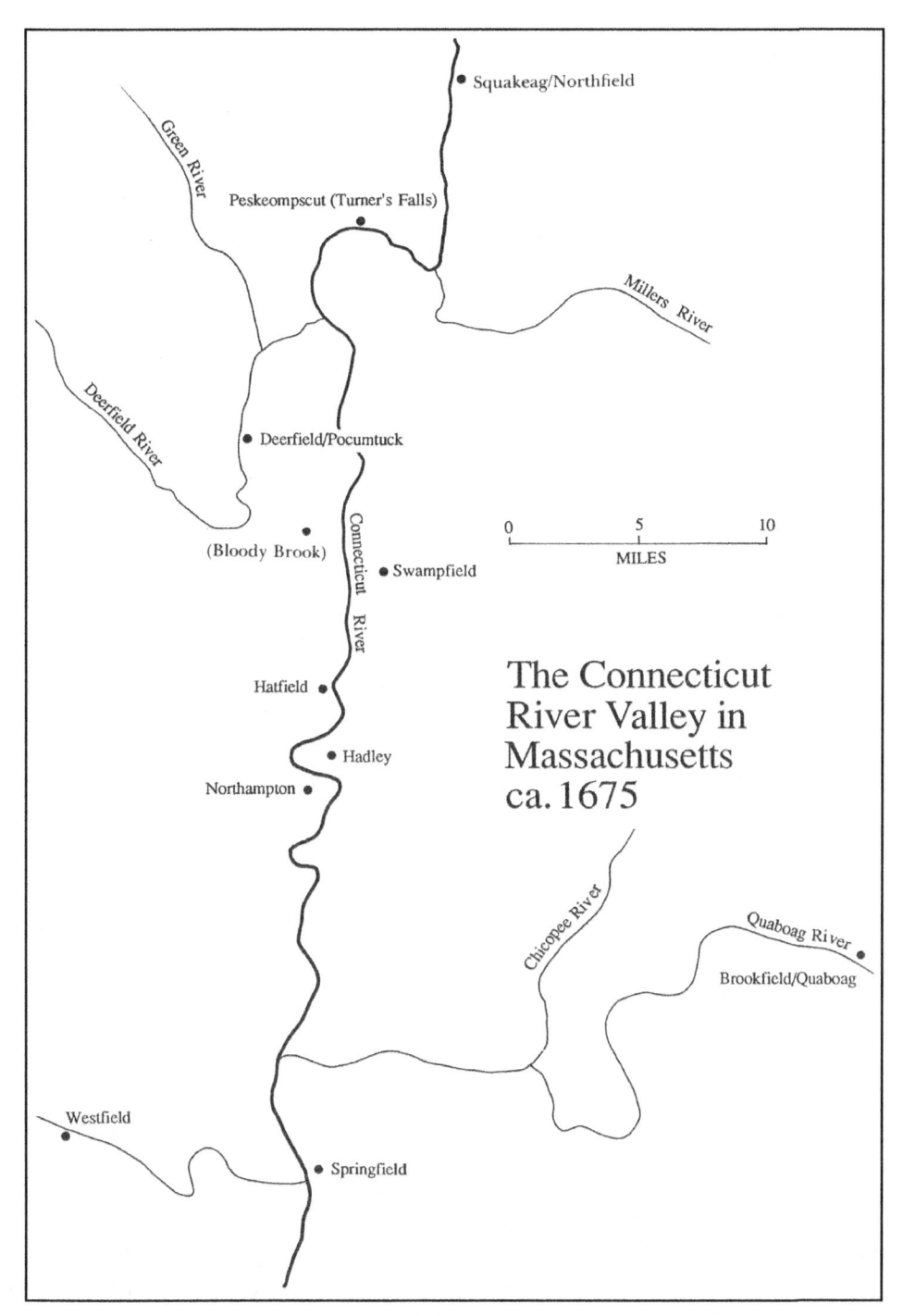

Map 2: Connecticut River Valley
(Melvoin 70)

Return to Deerfield

In the Spring of 1677 Benoni Stebbins married Mary Broughton, her [deceased] husband's dearest friend.[42]

With peace seemingly at hand, some of the Pocumtuck settlers driven away after Bloody Brook, returned to Deerfield and attempted to reestablish the village. Two of the original settlers, Sergeant John Plympton and Quintin Stockwell returned in spring 1677. They were joined by John Root, who had married the widow of one of Hinsdale's sons, and 22-year-old Benoni Stebbins, who took up a plot of land purchased years earlier by his [grand] father, Rowland. In the summer they were joined by Philip Mattoon, who settled on the land he rented from John Pynchon, one of the community's largest landholders." On the 19th of September 1677, the Indians attacked. "John Root was killed; they also took a number of prisoners, including Benoni Stebbins who subsequently escaped."[43]

The next day the party traveled northward and about 30 miles beyond Northfield encamped for three weeks. Some eighty Indian women and children from Wachusett joined them; they being part of the emigration of Massachusetts Indians to Canada:[44]

> As Capt. Salisbury wrote, 'God in His Providence hath sent us one of o'r captivated men, Benoni Stebbins by name, w'ch is ye occaision of these lines to yo'rself... So desire ye to put ye Macquas upon Psueing their and our enemys, there being greate likelihood of their overtaking them. Benoni Stebbins came into Hadley last night in ye night, whose relation was sent to me, w'h being but an hour since I had it, I Psently resolved upon sending Post to you.'[45]

Indian alarms were frequent; although the village was more or less under the protection of Albany and of those friendly Indians who came a-hunting over the Mohawk Trail.[46]

For two weeks the distracted people of Hatfield knew nothing of their friends; then Benoni Stebbins, having escaped, brought them tidings. He said that the Indians had 'been encouradged that they should have eight pounds apiece' for the captives, and that the French Indians intended 'to come with them the next time... if they had sucses this time.'[47]

After 19 Sept 1677 and after Benoni's escape, the council was wrong in this case, for the Indian attackers were not Mohawks, as Pocumtuck native Benoni Stebbins learned during his march and captivity. The 26 Indians in the band, 18 of whom were fighting men, were 'Norwooluck' Indians, plus one Narragansett, all natives of southern New England led by Asphelon. This suggests that the native survivors of King Philips War had attacked as an act of revenge, an ominous sign for the colonists of the valley. Also ominous was the fate of the prisoners. The Indians killed 3, and Pocumtuck's Sgt Plympton died horribly, burned at the stake. Stebbins said the Indians fled north to the French and lived there after King Philips war.[48]

Settlers taken captive from Hatfield/Deerfield in King Phillips War:

1677

Stebbins, Benoni
Stockwell, Quentin
Root, John
Plympton, Sergeant John
Russell, Samuel
      (Coleman 2:43)

Chapter 3

THE STRANGE DEATH OF JOHN STEBBINS, SENIOR

According to the following historical account[1], Benoni and John Jr's father met an untimely, strange end:

> The manner of his death was considered quite unusual, and the common belief was that he had been killed by witches. He was part owner of a sawmill on Broad Brook or Manhan River, and the facts would seem to indicate that he came to his death by an accident at the mill. There is a tradition that "while sawing at his mill, the logs would roll over him, set in motion by witches, by which he was severely bruised". An inquest was held by a jury of twelve men, who returned a verdict, which, while it did not directly charge witchcraft, showed that they more than half believed it had something to do with his death. Two examinations were made of the remains, and two reports were handed in to the court. In the first one they declared that there was a "warmth and heate in his Body yt dead persons are not usual to have"; and that there were "fower places upon his brest yt seemed to have been Pintched, though the doctor informed ym that in his life time there was a swelling between the Pintches"; his neck was as flexible as that of a living person; upon his body were found "several hundred of spots," that looked as if "they had been shott with small shott," and when they were scraped there

were holes under them. On the second examination, which must have been made soon after the first one, they found, as would very naturally follow, "the body somewhat more cold yn before, his joynts more limber," and several bruises on different pai-ts of his person, which they had not previously discovered. The jury reported to the County Court in April, and Samuel Bartlett, brother-in-law to Mr. Stebbins, and who seems to have been witch-finder in general for the town, brought in all the testimony he could obtain. It was also stated that a large number of women were summoned by Joseph Hawley, to examine and touch him, intending in this way to discover the witch. Blood flowed when a certain woman touched him, but only one could see it, so nothing was done.

This evidence, which cannot now be found, was sent to the Court of Assistants at Boston, but no further action was taken. Undoubtedly the testimony pointed to some suspected person, but no one was named on the records.

Chapter 4

PERMANENT SETTLEMENT

Benoni's wife, Mary, appears to have been a kindred spirit. In 1678 she was presented by the County Court, and fined 10 shillings for "wearing silk contrary to law" and aggravating the offense 'by persisting in it after she was once presented before.'[1] 'Benoni Stebbins, openly affronted the court and said 'he would not pay the money due for fees to the clerk of the Court'; this Court adjudged him to 'pay as a Fine to the court 10 sh. forthwith and committed him to the constable for the payment of the aforesaid fines.'[2]

The first step in making Deerfield a permanent settlement was taken in October 1678:

> Oct. 1678. In ans[r] to the petition of the remayning inhabitants of Deerefield, the court judgeth it meete to referr the peticoners to the proprietors for attayning of their interest, so farr as they shall judge necessary, leaving y[e] matter wth the Comittee to regulat; improvements & charges to be levyed thereupon, as shall judge legall & meete, for the encouraging the rebuilding of that plantation.[3]

On Dec. 12th 1680 a meeting of the Committee Proprietors to promote the settling of Deerfield was held in Northampton. The only action known, was the "granting to Thomas Hastings seven cow commons, likewise to David Hoite six cow commons, and to Samuel Field six cow commons. In May 1681, their appointment was confirmed by the General Court.[4]

In 1682 the permanent settlement began. "Among the very first of those by whom the town was permanently established, were John Sheldon and his wife's [Hannah] brothers, John and Benoni Stebbins.'"[5]

By 1684, Benoni had longest criminal record: 1676 fine for wife wearing silk, he refused thus getting his own fine, 1680 non-payment of debt to John Pynchon, 1682 non-payment to Joseph Parsons of Springfield, 1684 failure to properly care for his apprentice.[6]

Benoni Stebbins returned with his wife, Mary, and their children, Ebenezer and Thankful. John Jr. "remained a few years in vicinity of Boston, working at the trade of a carpenter. There he married Dorothy Alexander, daughter of John Alexander, a Scotsman, but returned at the Permanent Settlement" in Deerfield.[7] In August 1685, "home lots were granted to Benj. Barrett and James Brown; and soon after to Thomas Broughton, Benjamin and Samuel Hastings, John and Benoni Stebbins, Benjamin and Jonathon Church, Joseph Bodman, Ebenezer and Nathaniel Brooks, Robert Alexander, Martin Smith, Ephraim Beers, Joseph Gillette and Thomas Hurst. These grants were generally made on condition of being built upon within a year, and maintaining all abutting meadow fence. This little band consisted of young men, nearly all with wives and young children, seeking permanent home in this fertile valley. Their social relations were intimate, being closely connected by blood or marriage. The Brooks were brothers and Benoni their brother-in-law. The Stebbins were brothers, while John was brother-in-law to Alexander and Barrett, and the latter, brother-in-law to Benjamin Hastings."[8] Capt. Wells and Sgt. Benoni are the only 2 men with over 20 cow commons shares.[9]

Benoni Stebbins returned with his wife, Mary, and their children, Ebenezer and Thankful. "Indian alarms were frequent; although the village was more or less under the protection of Albany and of those friendly Indians who came a-hunting over the Mohawk Trail."[10]

With Benoni and Mary, came his brother John and his family, and the family of Benoni's old partner in crime, Godfrey Nims. Before he had turned 40, this former juvenile delinquent had served four times as a selectman, was a sergeant in the militia, and had become one of the wealthiest men in town. His house stood on the west-side of the street between those of Ensign Shelton, his brother-in-law, and the local minister."[11]

As before, growing families and the hope of betterment and economic security drew settlers to take up lands in this exposed frontier village. Proprietary shares could be bought from those who had grown discouraged and from heirs of those who had died in the war. If a man could not afford to buy rights to land, the town granted him twenty acres and a home lot. In return, a recipient had to take up the land and remain for three years. Again, those who were attracted by these conditions tended to be relatively young heads of newly established families. Among the new settlers, two-thirds of the adults were in their twenties or early thirties. Half of the family units contained three people or fewer; a dozen were single males. Overwhelmingly, these men and women were first-generation New England born. The men came from families in which a majority of the men had had to leave their hometowns to find new lands on which to establish their families.[12] Many of these settlers became the young, new leaders of Deerfield. Being one of Deerfield's first elders, a farmer like his neighbors, Benoni commanded the respect of his peers who referred to him by his title – Sgt. Stebbins.

Benoni Stebbins, who escaped when the war partly led by Ashpelon attacked Deerfield, was the final member of Deerfield's new circle of leaders. He was a colorful character originally from Northampton, whose life story shows that one did not have to be a devout Puritan to succeed in New England. Spirit and force of personality, not piety or education set him apart.[13]

Around 1680 at an early age when most new Englanders turned to older men, they led the local militia and filled half the positions on the board of selectman during the period before 1704. But they did command respect among status-conscious New Englanders who deferred their judgement and regularly referred to them by their titles: Captain Wells, Deacons Hoyt and Sheldon, Mister Catlin, and Sgt. [Benoni] Stebbins.[14]

Another notable leader in the town, the Reverend John Williams, held a center stage spot in the tale that is about to unfold. As Deerfield's pastor, John Williams, a 22-year-old Roxbury resident and recent graduate of Harvard College, had had the metal to accept the call to this frontier village where life would not be as easy as it was for ministers in more established towns. Two other candidates had turned down the job before Williams accepted the invitation to settle in 1686. His call came from the town, as well as the church, for it was the town's taxpayers – those outside of the church

Reverend John Williams
(Sweeney 4)

as well as full members – who paid the minister's salary. As in most other New England towns, the minister's salary was the highest single item in the local budget.

49

Though poor, Deerfield's residents tried to be generous. They agreed to pay Williams a salary of 60 pounds a year, to be raised eventually to 80 pounds, which would put him on a par with the ministers of Hadley and Northampton. In addition, they gave him a home lot in the center of town, built him a sizable house, gave him land in the open fields, and provided him with proprietary shares in future land divisions. The community and John expected that his pastoral relationship would endure for life and that the spiritual growth and well-being of both parties would intertwine.[15]

As minister, John Williams was one of the most prominent settlers in Deerfield. His status was reflected in the unusual structure of his household, which included Deerfield's few African-American residents. Like several other New England ministers, Williams was a slave owner. The presence of slaves, who provided household labor, made clear that even frontier Deerfield was connected to the networks of trade and bound labor that defined the economy of the Atlantic world. Williams first slave, known as Robert Tigo, possibly an Anglicized version of the name Roberto Santiago, appears to been an African who came to Deerfield from a Portuguese or Spanish colony. In the late 17th century few slaves came directly from Africa to New England. Most were transported north from the Caribbean basin to Rhode Island for resale. After Tigo's death, Williams purchased a man and a woman named Frank and Parthenia. Their names reveal little about their possible origin, for which there is no other evidence.[16]

On the 16th of December 1686 Thomas Wells was chosen Moderator:

> Wm Smead, Joshua Pumry, Jno Sheldon, Benoni Stebbins, Benj. Hastings and Thomas French were chosen Selectman Townsmen or Overseers to continue in office until oth*s* be chosen and they discharged according to law.[17]

On the vacation of the Charter, Dudley was made royal Governor in 1686. He was succeeded the next year by Sir Edmund Andros, who was put at the head of all the New England colonies by the Catholic King James. Andros being tyrannical and oppressive in his administration, aroused much opposition. He was of French extraction, and there was a strong undercurrent of feeling that he favored the Roman Catholics, and was intriguing to transfer these colonies to French dominion. On 12th of April 1689, the Prince of Orange had landed in England. On the 18th, Andros was seized by the people and imprisoned, with his principle adherents. The government was assumed by a Committee of Safety, which on the 2d of May issued a call for the towns to choose representatives to meet in Boston on the 9th. There is no record of any meeting here [Deerfield] in response to this call. The people, however, were ripe for revolt, and the Selectman stepped at once to the front, assuming the grave responsibility.[18] The State archives provide a hint:

> 'We, the Town of Deerfield, complying with the desire of the present Councell of Safety to choose one among us as a representative, a person, who will signify our minds and concurrence with the Councell for the establishing of the government', have chosen and deputed Lieutenant Thomas Wells, and signified to him our minds for proceeding to the settlement of the government, as hath been signified to us by the Honorable Councell of Safety, and those other representatives.[19]

This was signed by the four Selectman, including Benoni and meant that if the revolution failed, Wells could be court martialed at the hands of a vindictive Governor Andros and punished for treason along with the rest of us.

During this time, Benoni Stebbins's wife, Mary, clung to life for two months after she bore twins, but she succumbed on April 2, 1689.[20] After the war, in another event, Ebenezer Stebbins, son of Benoni, was a dragoon in the band of troopers that pursued the Indians, July 14, 1698. This was known as the "Pomeroy Pursuit".[21]

Chapter 5

KING WILLIAM'S WAR

King William's War (1689–97), as it was known in North America, was a war between Colonial New England and New France. Because neither England nor France thought of weakening their position in Europe to support the war effort in North America it was essentially confined to areas bordering the northeastern colonies. The war resulted from the deposition of Catholic King James II, allowing Protestants William and Mary to take the throne. William allied with the League of Augsburg to fight France where James had gone for exile. In North America this resulted in a series battles between the Northern Colonies, allied with the Iroquois, and New France allied with the Wabanaki Confederacy. The battles were over the border between New England (whose charter included the Maine area) and New France (whose definition of Acadia was defined as including portions of Maine). New France and the Wabanaki Confederacy were able to thwart New England expansion into Acadia, whose border was the Kennebec River in southern Maine. The strengthened relationship between New France and its Wabanaki Confederacy allies became a factor in Queen Anne's War.[1]

King William III
(Drake 1)

Queen Mary
(Drake 4)

With the recommendations of Lieut. Thomas Wells for increased security after the massacre at Schenectady, the town voted on Feb. 26 1689-90:

Att a Leagall Town meeting Feb^r 26th 1689-90

That y^r shall be a good sufficient fortification made upon the meeting hous hill: it was voted in the affirmative

For the stating proportioning and dividing to every p^{r}son his part or proportion of fortification: for stating the height flankrs gates &c the Town have made choice of M^r jn^o Catlin, Jonath Wells, Samuel Northam, Benj Barret, Thos French, Henry White and Benoni Stebbins to act and doe in every part and particular as to ye p^{r}mises as y^a shall Judg for ye good benefit & safety of the Town: voted in ye affirmative

Thatt ye fortifications shall be don & finished by ye 8th of March next emediately ensueing: voted affirmatively

Thatt all persons whose families cannot conveniently and comfortably be received into ye houses y^t are already upon ye meeting hous and hill shall be wthn the fortifications: such persons shall have habitations provided for y^m wthn s^d fortifications att the Town charg but any p^{r}son or p^{r}sons y^t shall provide habitations for y^{m}selves shall be exempt from ye charges afores^d: voted in the affirmative

That Sgt Jno Sheldon, Benoni Stebbins & Edward Allyn shall have full pow^r to appoint where every persons hous or cellar shall stand w^t bigness y^a shall be: y^t is such houses or cellars as are to be built by ye town as afores^s: voted in the affirmative.[2]

On December 26th 1692, Ens. Jno Sheldon, Ltt. David Hoyt, Sergt. Benoni Stebbins, Corp. Thomas French and Simon Beaman, were chosen selectmen fo the year ensuing. This vote shows the importance attached to military titles, and also, it may be the judgement of the people that the most efficient administration of affairs, in this time of distress, could be secured by a union of military and civil power.[3]

On March 11th 1692-3 it was voted "that the meeting hous shall be new seated; that Deacon David Hoyt & Deacon Jno Sheldon shall be 2 of ye persons to doe it and

The Dead 1704

Ben⁰ Stebins to be wᵗʰ yᵐ in sᵈ work."[4]

On March 7ᵗʰ 1698:

That yᵉ persons for a Com'ity yᵗ yᵉ Town did chose and empower in ye carrying on yᵉ school house aforesaid and in hiring a school master: were Mr. Jno Catlin, Benony Stebbins and William Armes…[5]

Settlers taken captive from the Hatfield & Deerfield area during King Williams War:

1693	1696
Smith, Martin	Gillette, John
	Belding, Daniel
	Nathaniel
	Hester or Esther
	(Coleman 2:43)

Chapter 6

THE SARAH SMITH AFFAIR

If all this were not enough, just as the tensions of war were finally easing in 1698, Deerfield suffered the most dramatic and perhaps terrible personal horror in its first half-century. The story of Sarah Smith brings together the dominant themes of Deerfield's life through this entire period – war, the pressures of the frontier, living a proper Puritan life, townspeople closely bound up with one another, living with sin, and living with death – and binds them together in a story of adultery and murder which ended with Western Massachusetts's first known public execution.[1]

Sarah Smith's origins are unclear. Local tradition would tie her to a family in Hadley where one Phillip Smith was 'murdered with a hideous witchcraft,' but there is no direct evidence to support this. All that is clear is that she was living in Deerfield with her husband, Martin, in 1693 when he was captured by 'Canada Indians.' Of Martin more is known. One of Pocumtuck's first settlers, as a young single man he got in trouble with the law in 1674 when he tried to kiss Jedediah Strong's wife and offered her 'some abuse.' After Bloody Brook he had moved to Northampton, yet returned early in the resettlement efforts, securing a home lot in 1682. Two years later he married Mary Phelps of Northampton; within a year of her death in 1692, he married Sarah. Although he served as a fence viewer in 1689, he left no record of further service to the town before his capture on October 13, 1693, near Wapping.[2]

From that point on Sarah was alone, for she had no children and her family apparently did not live in Deerfield. In the summer of 1694, she became a public figure, though hardly through a wish of her own. On the night of July 31 Deerfielder John Evans came to her house just outside the fort and talked with her for a few minutes. According to Ebenezer Stebbins [probably Benoni's son] and Henry White, two watchmen at the time, they said they had witnessed her rape and then 'they 'ran away

57

from that door' and did not speak out until five days later."[3]

No record has been found of what, if any, punishment John Evans suffered from this attempted rape. Nor is there any way to gauge the trauma that Sarah Smith felt as she continued alone, a young wife without family living in a besieged frontier town with her husband captured by Indians and probably dead. For three more years Smith lived under these conditions. Then came a new and greater tragedy. Sarah killed a bastard daughter from an alleged affair with another man, Joseph Cleeson. She was given a trial in Springfield and sentenced to 'be hanged by the neck until she be dead' on August 25, 1698. Just before the execution Reverend John Williams gave an extremely long lecture [64 pages] on her 'whoredom', murder, and adultery, those 'sins of darkness'."[4]

While we cannot condone the decisions she made, one could wonder about her subsequent mental state after losing her husband to the Indians and being assaulted with no recourse or support. In the end, her husband returned after five years of captivity in December 1698, about three months after her execution.

Chapter 7

QUEEN ANNE'S WAR:

The War of the Spanish Succession

On March 1st 1700, the school committee chosen, consisted of: "Mr. Jno p- -" Catlin, Sergt Jno Hawks and Jno Stebins" ***** "whose work shall be to hire a meet person or persons to teach ye Towns Children to Read and write as also to repair ye Towns School house at their discretion which is to be repaired at ye Towns Charge ; as also to proportion ye previding of firewood to ye Scholars.[1]

Queen Ann's War, as it was known here in the Colonies, developed as the result of a European conflict as follows:

The agreement that England and France had concluded at Ryswick in 1697 was more an armistice than a trade treaty. Both the actual fighting of the war and the settlement proved inconclusive. The reason for this was clear: Charles II of Spain, and aged, crippled, impotent, pathetic product of generations of royal inbreeding, was about to die without an heir. By 1697 Europe anxiously awaited his death and the determination of the fate of the Spanish Empire. When it finally came in 1700, Charles's death interrupted the negotiations between Louis XIV of France and William of Orange over the control of Spain and the dispensation of her overseas trade. When it was surprisingly announced that Charles had left a will, the negotiations broke down entirely. The will shook Europe and drove it

Queen Anne
(Drake 142)

once again into war.[2]

King Louis XIV
(Drake 145)

In essence, Charles had ceded the Spanish throne to Louis XIV via his grandson, duc d'Anjou, and further stipulated that if Louis did not take the crown it would go to the son of the Hapsburg emperor. Although Louis was not anxious to plunge into another war, he could hardly forgo the chance to gain control over the Spanish Empire, much less let such power slip from his hands to the rival Hapsburgs. Therefore, though he knew that accepting the will's terms would likely bring a resumption of war, he took the risk and accepted Spain for his grandson.[3]

England quickly responded. To oppose France and Spain, William brought together the "Grand Alliance," composed of much the same forces as he had led in 1689: England, Holland, Rome, Brandenburg, Portugal, and Savoy. Thus, began what became known in Europe as the war of the Spanish Succession.[4]

Or as Sheldon puts it:

Queen Anne's War begins after a relatively short period of peace for the Deerfield settlers. On September 16th, 1701, exiled James II of England, died in France, where his son, the 'Pretender', was at once proclaimed King of England, by the French Monarch, Louis XIV. William III, of England, resenting this insult and threat, formed a strong alliance with Austria and other powers against France, but he died soon after, March 8, 1702. His successor, Queen Anne, declared war against France May 4, 1702, and for more than 10 years Europe was convulsed to its center in a conflict to establish a balance of civil and ecclesiastical power. The scent of blood crossed the sea, and the English colonies soon felt the fury of Romish zeal and savage ferocity.[5]

As the northwestern-most town of New England, Deerfield, Massachusetts, found itself in 1704 at the forefront of a clash of peoples and empires in northeastern North America. Deerfield in February 1704 thus became a point of convergence for struggles that had both trans – Atlantic and local origins. Fighting had begun in the Northeast in 1703 as part of a major European war, the war of the Spanish Succession.[6]

On the peace of 1697, some of the settlers had left Meetinghouse Hill and located "some a mile and some two miles" away; now they are gathering again within the palisades.

> Att a legal Town meeting in Deerfield Sept 11: 1702: Ens. Jno Sheldon moderator The Town y^n agreed and voted y^t ye Comon field shall be opened on Wednesday in ye morning being ye 30th day of y^s instant September 1702 There was also at ye same meeting a little piece of land Granted to Sergint Jno Hawkes to builde in ye fort for his lifetime ; which land is to be in ye middle hieway leading into ye meadow and on ye south East corner of Mr. Jno Williams his home lot adjoining therevnto as it shall be laid to him by a Comitty:
>
> The Comitty Chosen for s^d work were Capt. Jonathan Wells, Liett David Hoyt and Sergeant Benony Stebins.[7]

French/Indian Motives

When war broke out in Europe in 1702, prospects for renewed war in North America rose quickly. In the lull between the storms – the five years of peace between New England and New France from 1697 to 1702 – both sides had moved to strengthen Indian alliances. By 1701 the French had succeeded. The English never wholly did.[8]

Native concerns in a conflict that had originated in Europe had ramifications for everyone in the Northeast. Haefelie and Sweeney explained it this way:

> Natives in the Northeast hesitated to involve themselves in this contest between the rival empires. They were still recovering from a long series of wars that had ended only a few years before. Despite long – standing problems with the English, many of the Abenakis and Pennacooks wanted to remain 'Neuters', but the strategic plans of the French and the fears and provocations of the English made neutrality impossible. Influenced by Imperial strategy and colonial trade, officials in New France precipitated the fighting by pressuring Eastern Abenakis and Pennacooks to attack English settlements in Maine in August 1703. But throughout the war, the less than enthusiastic native allies of the French often hung back from fights in which they had nothing to gain. Thanks in part to their efforts, peace always threatened to break out in the Northeast long before the war of the Spanish succession had ended in Europe.[9]

In his book, Calloway further writes about Haefelie and Sweeney:

> They take as their starting point a famous event, with Indians playing a familiar role – the raid on Deerfield, Massachusetts, in the winter of 1704, by Indian warriors and their French-Canadian allies. But Haefelie and Sweeney go beyond the familiar narratives of the raid and subsequent experiences of John and Eunice Williams. They place the event in the broader context of a northern New England borderland of interethnic complexity, and they search out the identities of the Abenaki, Mohawk, and Huron Indians involved. They find that many of the Indians had ties to the Deerfield region and even to the colonists they raided, and that all had compelling motives for participating in the infamous attack. They also demonstrate the connections that existed between different Indian communities in northern New England and Quebec in the wake of the diaspora of Indian peoples following King Phillips War.[10]

Abenaki Clothing
Eighteenth-century watercolor of an Abenaki woman and man by an unknown artist. Their clothing indicates the ways that Abenaki used European blankets and cloth to fashion distinctive costumes.
(Sweeney 6)

It should be noted that there are subtle differences between the terms used by historians, like Sheldon from a pre-1900 era where sentiments were still high, and the more 'multi-cultural' historians that exist today. The use of the word 'massacre by Sheldon and the use of the word 'raid' by Calloway and Haefeli & Sweeney illustrate this point.

Some of the 'true' French/Indian motives for the conflicts in New England are best illustrated by some of the communications after the 1704 attack.

Governor de Vaudreuil writes to the war minister at Paris, Nov.14th, 1703, that he should send a strong party against the English in the Spring, 'were it only to break up the measures the English might be adopting to induce the Abenaquis to conclude peace.'[11]

That the true motive of the expedition against Deerfield has been thus given, is shown by another letter from Vandreuil to the Minister, Nov. 16th, 1704, in which he speaks of 'the success of a party I sent this winter on the ice as far as the Boston government at the request of the Abenakis.' Charlevoix, in his history of New France, tells the story of an attack by the English on the Abenakis, whose:[12]

Phillipe de Rigand de Vaudreuil
(Haefeli & Sweeney 170)

> Chiefts called on M. Vaudreuil for aid, and he sent out during the winter 250 men commanded by the Sieur Hertel de Rouville *** who, in his turn, surprised the English, killing a large number of them, and took 150 prisoners. He himself lost only three Frenchmen, and some savages.[13]

In the letter of November 16th, quoted above, Vaudreuil commends de Rouville, and asks his promotion, complacently adding, 'Sieur de Rouvilles party, My Lord, has accomplished everything that was expected of it; for independent of the capture of a fort, it showed the Abenakis that they could truly rely on our promises; and this is what they told me at Montréal on 13th of June, when they came to thank me.'[14]

Thus, this representative of a Christian nation, sent an army through the wilderness, not to fight an English force, but to surprise and butcher the settlers of an English plantation three hundred miles away, merely to keep on good terms with a savage tribe, and gratify his own ambition. It was an act of hardly less than cold-blooded murder. De Rouville's command was made up of two hundred French, and one hundred and forty

Jean Baptiste Hertel de Rouville
(Haefeli & Sweeney 234)

Indians, part French Mohawks, or "Macquas" of Caghnawaga – probably in civilized dress – and part Eastern Indians in native costume. The oft-told tale that the Indians for love of their favorite valley, came back to punish the white intruders, is pure romance; for not a Pocumtuck or the son of a Pocumtuck appears on the scene. On the contrary, the Macques were the hereditary enemies of the Pocumtucks.[15]

Initial Preparations

Newly commissioned Governor Joseph Dudley brought news of the war when he arrived in Boston on June 11, 1702. During a Town meeting they began preparations for the expected hostilities. The Council in Massachusetts considered the threat of war to be ominously evident. Following Massachusetts law, local officers trained the town militia. The town was also required to have a 'sufficient watch house' and to maintain 'a watch,' a vigil of sentinels for the town. As of 1702, Deerfield did not have as many fortified houses as many other frontier towns – only three versus as many as 10 or 12 – but the town did have its palisade, or fort, enclosing the center of the town. This 'good and sufficient fortification' had been built in 1689, at the beginning of King William's War, and improved in 1697.[16]

Governor Joseph Dudley
(Drake 149)

In June the Town realized the need for action at the following town meeting:

> Att a legall Town meeting in Deerfield, June 26, 1702:
> Ens. Jno. Sheldon, moderator:
>
> That y^e Town fort shall forthwith be Righted vp. Voted affimatively
>
> That every man shall for ye present Right vp his proportion of ye fort ye was last laid out to him: Voted affirmatively.
>
> That all ye fort shall be Righted vp by Wednesday next at

night vpon penalty of 3 shillings p^r Rod for every Rod y^n Defective and after y^t one shilling per Rod so long as s^d fortification shall lie unrepaired: Voted afirm:

That ye comisioned officers shall be ye men y^t shall Inspect and pass ye fort in General: Voted affirm

That a pittion be sent to ye Gouerner for help and Relief in our present distress occaision by a prospect of war: The Town left ye wording of s^d petition with Capt Jonah Wells and Mr Jno Richards together with ye selectmen: Voted affirmatively:"[17]

In July, 1702, the Council responded with the following decree:

In the Council July 2d, 1702

Upon a representation made by inhabitants of Deerfield in the County of Hampshire, the most westerly frontier of the province, that a considerable part of the Line of Fortification about their Plantation is decayed and fal^n down, praying for some assistance in rebuilding and setting up the same, for that they are apprehensive of some evil designs forming by the Indians, an unwonted intercourse of Indians from other Plantations being observed.

Advised, that his Excellency do write to John Pynchon Esq. Coll. Of the Regiment of militia in that County, directing him forthwith to send his Lieut. Coll to Deerfield aforesaid to view the Palisado about that Town, and to stay there some short time, to put the Inhabitants upon the present repair of the said fortifications in all places where it is defective, and to cover them with a scout of ten men by turns out of the next towns whilst they are about said work, and to assure them of an necessary support and to take the like order as to Brookfield saving the scout. The scout not to be paid. [Six soldiers were paid 65 pounds for this service.][18]

At subsequent Town meetings, further preparatory actions were considered. "The house of John Wells, just outside the fort on the south end of town, was heavily fortified. The town selectmen were empowered to build up the "town stock of Ammunition." As in the 1690s the town also secured places inside the fort for all townspeople where they could sleep each night. Those with houses inside were required to shelter fellow townsmen, receiving a tax break for their pains. The town even gave "little pieces of land" inside the fort to at least two townsmen on which to build their own small houses.[19]

> Att a legall Town meeting in Deerfield Sept 11: 1702: Ens Jno Sheldon moderator The Town y^n agreed and voted y^t ye Comon field shall be opened on Wednesday in ye morning being ye 30th day of ye instant September 1702 There was also at ye same meeting a little piece of land Granted to Sergint Jno Hawkes to builde on in ye fort for his lifetime: which land is to be in ye middle hieway leading into ye meadow and on ye South East corner of Mr. Jno Williams his home lot adjoyning therevnto as it shall be laid to him by a Comitty:
>
> The Comitty Chosen for s^d work were Capt Jonathan Wells Liett David Hoyt and Sergeant Benony Stebins:[20]

Additional meetings continued on the same theme, run by the military leaders in the town. In December, 1702:

> Dec^{mb} 24:1702; Ens Jno Sheldon moderator The Town y^n agreed and voted y^t all timber or firewood y^t shall be only fal^n and not cut vp shall be forfeited at any yime after hath lain fal^n 3 months.[21]

Deerfield was wise to take these precautions, for the middle of 1703 there were ominous signs that war might soon strike the town. As early as May of 1703, even before the attacks on Wells and Saco, New York governor Cornbury sent notice to the Massachusetts governor Dudley that 'a party of French and Indians, near 100, maybe expected every day at Deerfield'. Dudley quickly alerted the town to 'be in readiness

Henry R. Stebbins Jr.

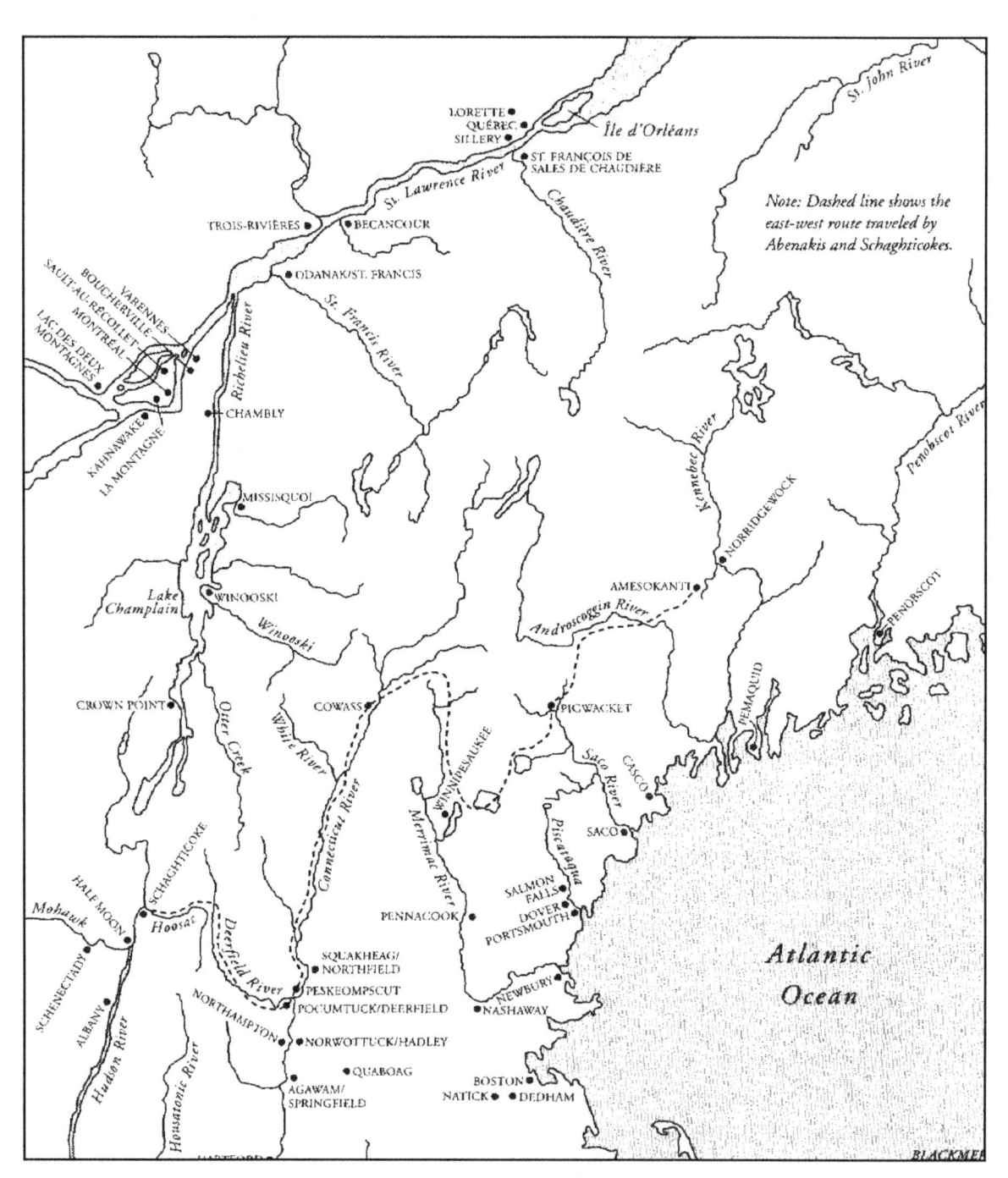

Map 3: The Northeast
circa 1660-1723
(Haefeli & Sweeney 13)

and to scout and range for a discovery'. Dudley also communicated the information to Connecticut governor Fitz-John Winthrop, both as a precaution for his colony and because Massachusetts again expected Connecticut to help defend the upper Valley. Winthrop felt that such an attack would be 'a bold attempt at this tyme', with war still only smoldering, and especially at Deerfield, a place 'soe remote & hazardous' from Québec. Still, counseling 'tis best to have an eye upon them," he urged preparedness and all frontier towns."[22]

Continued warnings from various sources trickled down to Deerfield. Suspicions riding high, Frenchmen in Deerfield were often considered spies for Canada. Lord Cornbury, the Governor of New York, sent a Message to Governor Dudley that Indian spies in his employ had determined that a military force was forming in Canada. A Major Peter Schuyler sent similar information to Dudley, resulting in a reinforcement of 20 soldiers from nearby towns.

Colonel Peter Schuyler
(Drake 280)

Preliminary Action

Finally, on the evening of October 8 the first blow of Queen Anne's war struck the Valley – at Deerfield. While they were watching after the town's animals in the pasture outside the fort, Indians ambushed Zebediah Williams and John Nims. After firing but missing, the Indians quickly seized Williams. Nims ran away toward a pond nearby, but then, afraid he would be shot, he gave himself up. The Indians quickly marched the men off to captivity.[23]

Deerfield's Cry for Support

Letters outlining Deerfield's poor status are given here in their entirety, not only as presenting pictures of the sad condition of our town, but because they contain much of value from other points of view.

In late October of 1703, the town's plight spurred its minister, Reverend John Williams, to write a poignant appeal for aid to Governor Dudley. Williams thanked the governor for his 'care and concernment for our safety', both in helping rebuild the fort and in supplying soldiers the previous year. Yet, Williams explained, now 'we have been driven from our houses & home lots into the fort, (where there are but 10 house lots in the fort). With some settlers moving a mile some 2 miles to live in the fort, the town had suffered much loss… we have in the alarms several times been wholly taken off from any business, the whole town kept in, our children of 12 or 13 years and under we have been afraid to improve in the field in fear of the enemy… we have been crowded together into houses to the preventing of indoor affairs being carried on to any advantage… so that our losses are far more than would have paid our taxes'.[24]

The pay of Massachusetts garrison soldiers was 5 shillings per week, as established by order in Council, May 29th, 1703. It had become a question whether our fortifications were strong enough to resist an attack, and a town meeting was called for Oct. 15th, 1703.[25]

> The Town at sd meeting Considering there nesasaty of fortifing agree & voted yt a comitty should be chosen to ioyn with Colonell patrigg to consult agree & determin wheither to fortifi or no and if Ye agreed to fortifie then in what manar place or places the committee to said work were: Capt. Wells: Lieut. Hoyt: Ensign John Sheldon: and Daniel Belden:[26]

Seeking any assistance from the colony, Williams continued:

> Strangers tell us they would not live where we do for 20 times as much as we do… several say they would freely leave all they have & go away were not that it would be disobedience to authority &… discouraging [to] their brethren. The frontier difficulties of a place so remote from

others and so exposed as ours, are more than be known, if not felt.[27]

The alarms caused by the news of hostilities in Maine was now increased ten-fold. Military affairs in Connecticut were put into the hands of a Council of War, with authority to defend Hampshire county as well as their borders. By the following paper, it would appear that a garrison of sixteen men, probably from Connecticut, was continued here through the season:

> An account of Billets of Sixteen Soldiers at the Garrison in Deerfield, from the 21st of October, 1703 to the sixth of December following, amounted to 6 pounds, 3 shillings, 5 pence having been examined by your Commisary General, was presented.[28]

The following modest, ingenuous and pathetic letter, gives a vivid picture of our settlement at this time. It was addressed:

> For his Excellency Joseph Dudley Esq. her Majesties Govenor for the Prounce of Massachusetts Bay in N. E. &c at his dwelling house In Roxb:
>
> Deerf. October 21, 1703.
>
> May it please your Excellency:
>
> As i am bound in duty i would thankfully knowledge your care and concernment for our safety in the Seasonal provision to get the fortifications made up, & in the care to have a supply of soldiers with us, so i am emboldened to lay before your Excellency our distress[d] state & condition, knowing your forwardness to commiserate & encourage frontiers, that you may stir up your Councele & Assembly to and encouraging of them, i would be far from showing any discontented complaint; an evil to common & frequent, to the dishonor of God, the scandal of religion, and the great exercise of them that are in place of power: yet I

Henry R. Stebbins Jr.

would lay open our case before your Excellency as it is; we have been driven from our houses & home lots into the fort, (there are but 10 house lots in the Fort). Some a mile some 2 miles, whereby we have suffered much loss, we have in the alarms several times been wholly taken off from any business, the whole town kept in, are children of 12 or 13 years and under we have been afraid to improve in the field for fear of the enemy, (our town plat & meadows all lay exposed to the view of an enemy if they come at any time on the mountains). we have been crowded together into houses to the preventing of indoor affairs being carried on to any advantage, & must be constrained to expend at least 50 pounds to make any comfortable provision of housing if we stay together in cold weather: so that our losses are far more than would have paid our taxes; the people have been very ready and forward to pay their taxes, & know sensibly that the present circumstances of the country call for & require great taxes, & would not in the least grumble, but i lay it before your Excellency, to move your Compassions of us: Strangers tell us they would not live where we do for twenty times as much as we do, the enemy having such an advantage of the river to come down upon us, several say they would freely leave all they have & go way were it not that it would be disobedience to authority & a discouraging their bretheren and: The frontier difficulties of a place so remote from others & so exposed as ours, are more than be known, if not felt. i am very sensible that if they have no ease as to their rates under the circumstances, the people must suffer very much; when the Country abated them their rates formerly, i was yet moved from certain knowledge of their poverty and distress, to abate them of my salary for several years together, tho they never askt it of me; & now their children must either suffer for want of clothing, or the Country consider them, or i abate them what they are to pay me: I never found the people unwilling to do when they had the ability, yea a they have often done above their ability; I would request

your Excellency so far to commiserate, as to do what may be encouraging to persons to venture there all in the frontiers, there charge will necessarily be trebled, if this place be deserted: i would humbly beg they may be considered in having something allowed them in the making the fortification: we have mended, it is in vain to mend & must make it all new, & fetch timber for 206 rod, 3 or 4 miles if we get oak: the sorrowful parents, & distress^d widow of the poor captives taken from us, request your Excellency to endeavor that there may be an exchange of prisoners to their release; i know i need not use arguments to move your Excellen^{ys} pitty and compassion of them & endeavors to have them returned: the blessings of them y^t are ready to perish will surely come upon you, in endeavors of this kind: i pray God direct and every way assist & encourage your Excellency in the great work before you, in a day of so great exercise & trial as this: my duty to yourself and Good Lady, with due respects to your Honorable family, requesting forgiveness for any failure in my writing as exercising your patience, begging prayers for me & mine, i rest your Excellency humble servant,
  John Williams:

[P.S. on the back.]

The people of the town earnestly requested me to draw something to present to your Excellency & assembly in their behalf & desire this may be presented in their name both to yourself, Council & Representatives.

Your Excellency's humble servant.

[Mass Archives, 113-350]

Rev. Solomon Stoddard to Gov. Dudley:

  Excellenct S^r

Henry R. Stebbins Jr.

The town of Deerfield has suffered much formerly from the Indians: of late two of their young men are car. into Captivity: this makes a great impression on the Spirits of the people & they are much discouraged. This puts it upon me to make two proposals to your Excellency –

The first is that they may be put in a way to Hunt the Inds. with dogs – Other methods have been taken are found by experience to be chargeable, hazardous and insufficient: But if dogs were trained up to hunt Inds. as th do Bears; we sh. quickly be senseble of a great advantage thereby. The dogs would be an extream terrour to the Inds; they not much afraid of us, they know they can take us – & leave us, if they can but get out of gun-shot, th count themselves in no great danger, however so many pursue them they are neither afraid of being discovered or pursued; But these dogs would be such a terrour to them, that after a little experience it w^d prevent their comming & men would live more safely in their houses & work more safely in the fields and woods: In case the Inds sh. come near the Towne the dogs w^d readely take their track & lead us to them: Sometimes we see the track of one or two Inds but cant follow it; the dogs would discover it and lead our men directly to their enemies; for want of w^h help we many times take a good deal of pains to little purpose – Besides if we had dogs fitted for that purpose our men might follow Inds w^h more safety, there would be [no?] hazzard of their being shot at out of the bushes, they would follow their dogs with an undaunted spirit, not fearing a surprise; & indeed the presence of dogs would very much facilitate their victory: the dogs would do a great deal of execution upon the enemy, & catch many and Indian that w^d be too light a foot for us.

If it should be thot by any that this way is impractible & that dogs would not [deavor?] to do what we expect from them, these two things may satisfy them, one is that in a time of war with Inds in Virginia, they did in this way prevail over them, though all attempts before they betook themselves to this method proved in vain; the other is that our Hunters give an account the dogs that are used to hunt Bears, mind no other track but the track of a Bear; from whence they may conclude that if dogs were used to pursue Indians they would mind nothing else.

If the Indians were as other people are, and did manage their warr fairly after the manner of other nations, it might be looked upon as inhumane to persue them in such a maner. But they are to be looked upon as theives and murderers, & they doe acts of hostility, without proclaiming war, they don't appear openly in the field to bid us battle, they use those cruelly that fall into their hands, they act like wolves, & are to be dealt withall as wolves.

There must be some charge in prosecuting this design, something must be expended for purchasing suitable dogs, & their maintenance, the men who spend their time and this service must be paid, but this will not rise in any proportion to the charge of maintaining a suitable number of garrison soldiers – I have taken advice with several of the principal persons among us & they looke upon this way as the most [favorable?] expedient in this case.

The other proposal is that the town of Deerfield may be freed from Country Rates during the time of war; their circumstances doe call for commiseration: sometimes they are alarmed & called off from their businesse, sometimes they dare not goe into the fields & when they doe goe, they are fain to wait till they have a gard; they can't make improvement of their outlands, as other Towns doe, their houses are so crowded, sometimes with soldiers, that men and women can doe little businesse within doors, & their spirits are so taken up about their Dangers, that they had a little heart to undertake what is needful for advancing their estates; it seems to be a thing acceptable to God, that they should be considered & freed from Rates; Your Excellency will not take it amiss that I take my accustomed freedom & am so over officious as to tender my advice before it is asked.

The good Lord guide y^r Ex'cy & the Genrl Assembly; to do that w^h shall be

serviceable to this afflicted Country w^n is the hearty prayer of your humble servant.

       Solo: Stoddard

North Hampton October 22, 1703.[29]

One result of this of the consultation ordered above appears in the following position petition:

To his Excellency, Joseph Dudley, Esq. Capt Genl and Govr over this Province of the Massachusetts Bay & to y^r Counsell & Representatives in Gen Corte assembled this 27 Oct. 1703. The town of Deerfield who lye much exposed to ye present enemy, wth obstructe them much in their occasions, their Lives hanging in doubt everywhere w^n they goe out. Also they are now forced to rebuild their fortifications at much disadvantage to them, & it being 320 rod or upwards, will fall very heavy to do it all upon their own charge, were verry earnest with me w^n lately there, to plead with this Corte for some allowance towards the doing of it out of their publique Rates now to be collected there; as also, that they might be Quitted of Rates to Y^e publique for y^e tyme being of this present warr, w^h it is so destressing upon them.

Saml Partridge[30]

The Dead 1704

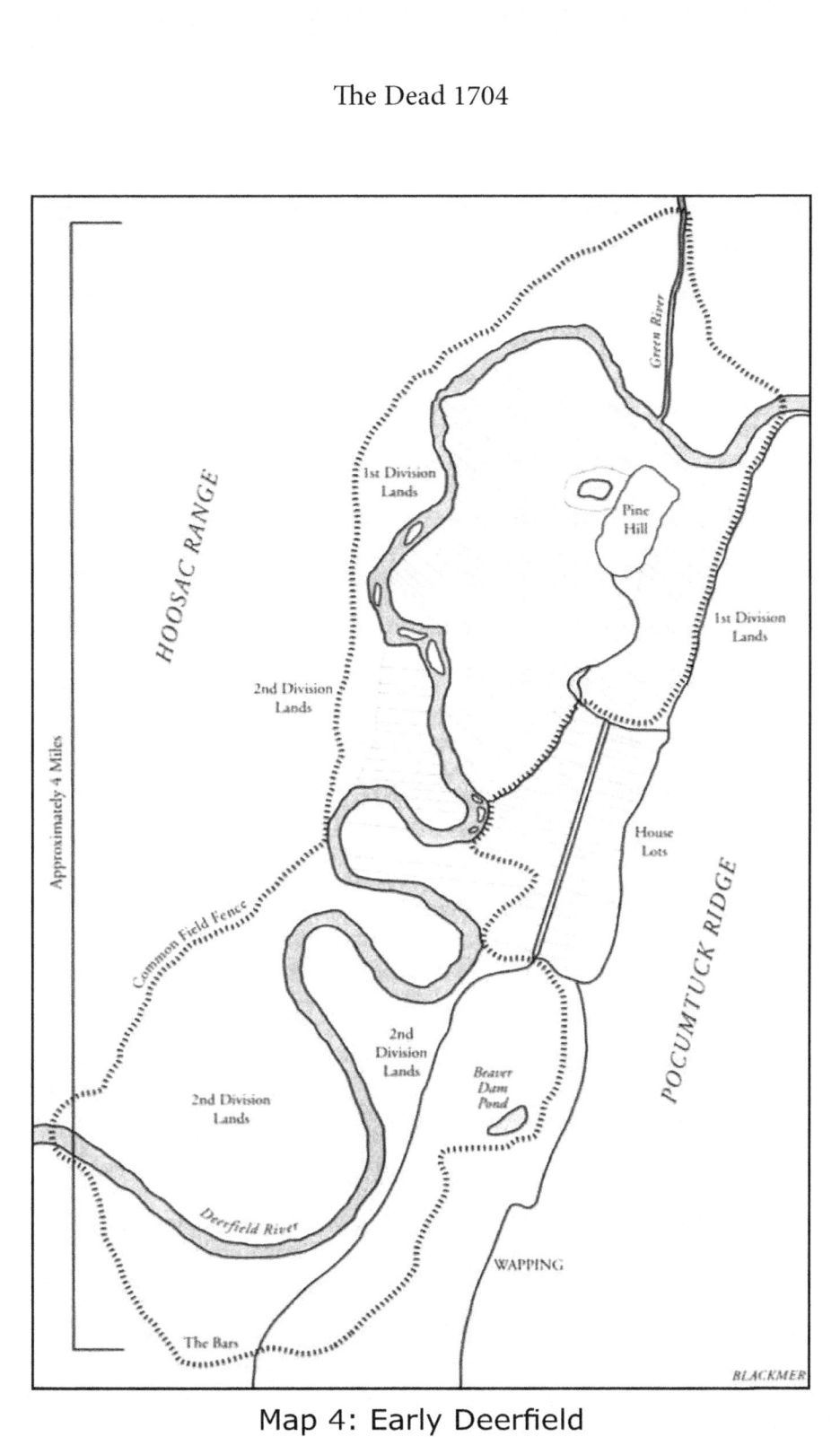

**Map 4: Early Deerfield
circa 1700**
(Haefeli & Sweeney 17)

Massachusetts heard Deerfield's cry. Not only did the General Court exempt the town from taxes for 1703 and sent money to support the ministry, but in late October it sent 16 more soldiers as well. As the snows of early winter came to the valley, however, these soldiers went home. Winter was not a time of fighting, certainly not a time of invasion by forces coming from 300 miles away. As military leader, John Pynchon had written on an early December day during King William's War, 'Y^e approaching winter gives hope of some respit & allowance of some Ease… The entering upon Winter wil give som security, for in Reson noe attempt can be fro[m] Canida now at this season.' Then he added one eerily prophetic line: 'tho when winter is setled al Rivers strong [frozen], Passage good, days lengthen and warmer weather – 'then may be ye Enemys motion.'[31]

By the statement of Col. Partridge, it is seen that 320 rods of Palisading were required. Mr. Williams says 206 is required. In 1693 "the whole compass of the Fort was 202 rods." Perhaps the present plan was to enclose with stockades the houses of Capt. Wells and Lieut. Hoyt, as places of refuge in sudden alarms – they were both well situated for that purpose, south and north of the main fort – and not unlikely to add flankers to the latter. There is no evidence of any works on at Hoyt's, but when the shock came, the stockading of Wells's house proved the salvation of many.[32]

This letter and the following from the Northampton minister, doubtless accompanied the petition of Partridge, and both were written for the same end. There seems to be a good deal of force in Stoddard's recommendation to train dogs to track the enemy, particularly in the suggestion that the men, being relieved from the danger of ambush, could follow the savages so much more efficiently. A practical objection, however, may have existed in the difficulty of teaching the dogs to distinguish between the enemy, and the friendly Indians employed as scouts.[33]

> Since I wrote: the father of the two Captives [Godfrey Nims] belonging to Deerfield, has importunately desired me to write to ye Ex'cy that you w^d endeavor the Redemption of his children – I request that if you have any opportunity, you w^d not be backward to such a work of mercy.[34]

The Assembly record for Nov. 26th, 1703, contains the following:

> Considering the extraordinary impoverishing circumstances, the Town of Deerfield is under by Reason of the

> present War, Resolved, that the sum of Twenty Pounds be allowed and paid out of the public Treasury towards the support of the ministry in the said Town of Deerfield for the y^r cur^t."[35]

The weeks dragged slowly on. The green ropes of summer had been changed to garments of scarlet and gold, among which the painted and plumed warrior could lurk unseen; but the town was unmolested. The blasts of autumn had laid this gaudy screen, seared and dry, upon the ground, forming a russet carpet, which not even the soft moccasined foot of the Indian could traverse undiscovered. The snow of winter piled unusually deep, and the wooded wilderness, stretching two hundred miles between the settlement and Canada, seemed a safe barrier: and with each changing season the feeling of security grew stronger. The settlers breathe more freely and gradually resumed their wonted ways of life, believing that the warnings of invasion were founded on unreliable reports.[36]

Even so, by February 20th Deerfield received news of probing attacks on Haverill and Exeter about 50 miles away. Worried about the danger, the regional commander, Samuel Partridge asked Connecticut governor Winthrop for soldiers. Deerfield received 20 soldiers that arrived around February 24th. Partridge's letter contained both hope and anxiety: 'through the goodness of God we are p'served yet and hope for respitt till ye rivers break up… but as soon as there be passing, we look for troubles.' Winter did not give Partridge, or Deerfield, their desired 'respitt.' Even as the 20-man garrison was arriving at Deerfield, an army of 200 to 300 French and Indians was moving south toward Deerfield.[37]

Stebbins Connection with the Frenchmen and Illegal Fur-trade

Long before the raiders gathered at Chambly headed south, three Frenchmen arrived in Deerfield. The suspicious descendants of Deerfield's colonial inhabitants along with later historians have often regarded these freshmen as possible spies. But unlike two Frenchman who had shown up in Deerfield late in 1702, the three new arrivals were not clapped in chains and taken to Boston. Jacques de Noyon and his unnamed companions were in fact *coureurs de bois,* renegade fur traders, who had previously been in contact with authorities in New York. If captured by the French, these men stood in greater danger of dying than any of the town's English residents. These men had fled to the English in search of economic opportunities denied to them because of the languishing condition of the Canadian fur trade. Their flight was symptomatic of the economic and diplomatic crisis in Canada, and actions such as there is concerned French officials who feared the loss of trade and possibly Native Allies. For their part, the inhabitants of Deerfield appear to have welcomed them into their community.[38]

Canadian Snowshoe Ranger
(Drake 47)

Jacques de Noyon had much in common with Hertel de Rouville and Renée Boucher de la Perriere. However, since he was not a nobleman, his connection to the French Empire was quite different from theirs. Like the officers, De Noyon had been born in Trois – Rivieres, that "cradle of explorers." In 1669 his father, a gunsmith, had moved the family to Boucherville, where Jacques grew up as a tenant of the Bouchers. But unlike his father, craftsman and farmer, he embraced the more adventuresome life of a fur trader. In 1688, he journeyed to the western shore of Lake Superior, where the French trader Daniel Greysolon Dulhut had erected a trading post. This point marked the farthest west that the French had traveled in the Great Lakes basin. Sometime in fall 1688 De Noyon paddled up the Kaministiquia River and spent the winter at Rainy Lake with a party of Assiniboines. In the spring he may have ventured even farther west before returning to Montréal. At some point De Noyon composed an account of his travels. Other traders and Canadian officials came to know of his exploits.[39]

Unlike most Raiders, De Noyon did not marry and settle down when he reached his late twenties. A man with a longing for adventure, not farming, he continued to travel to the Upper Country to trade for furs during the Nine Years War, financed by a succession of Montréal merchants. Boucherville was merely his home between trips west. So attached was he to his trade that he continued to travel to the Upper Country even after French authorities officially prohibited travel into the region in 1698. By the summer of 1700, De Noyon and a group of French traders who operated illegally in the West were "in a sort of rebellion." They informed English officials of their willingness to "come and trade with the English." Using an English captive living with the Ottawas as an intermediary, they approach the governor of New York, indicating that they wanted to settle in New York colony somewhere near the Iroquois. They hoped to bring with them some of the Ottawas who claimed that they too longed to trade with the English because "the French in Canada were not able to furnish [them] with goods.[40]

More loyal to this fur trade then the French, Jacques de Noyon was committing treason by proposing a plan that threatened to sever New France's lifeline to the fur trade of the Great Lakes. In October 1700 De Noyon and Louis Goselin, another renegade fur trader, traveled to New York and made a formal proposal to settle there. In return for "the same rights and privileges as others enjoy" in the town of Albany they pledged to "submit ourselves with promise of fidelity to the laws of the Government" and promised to return next year with other French fur traders "all laden with peltry" and ten or twelve of the principal sachems of the Ottawa nation. For French authorities such plans embodied their worst fears, because it came at a time when the Ottawas were, in fact, upset with the price that the French offered them for their furs. Because of Native understandings of the relationship between trade and alliance, diversion of furs to the English carried with it the possible loss of France's western allies. Just attempting to bring the Ottawas closer to Albany made De Noyon a dangerous man, even though there is no evidence that he delivered on his pledge.[41]

De Noyon's whereabouts for the next three years remained uncertain. By early 1704 he and two companions had been living in Deerfield "for some time," indicating that the town had links to New France that are not always well documented. Presumably he returned to the Ottawas and spent 1701 gathering furs. Sometime in 1702 or 1703 he left the Upper Country and arrived in Deerfield with two other Frenchman. The French already knew Deerfield as a way station for Iroquois captives being carried south, as a destination for deserters from the *troupes*, and as a place to trade. For these renegade fur traders, it may have provided a less conspicuous base of operations than did Albany, which was frequented by Frenchman and Natives from Canada involved in the illegal trade with the English. The ostensibly Catholic De Noyon gained enough acceptance in the New England town to marry seventeen-year-old Abigail Stebbins. The thirty-six-year-old French spinner of tales won the girl with stories of his wealth and position in New France.[42]

Greenlee describes the relationship between Jacques and the Stebbins family as follows:

> JACQUES DESNOIONS, a bushranger, discontented with his government and seeking a new home, went to Deerfield, Massachusetts. That he was thirty-six years old and unmarried, favors the theory that he had led a roving life. Flattered by the preference of the stranger, a man so much older than himself, ABIGAIL STEBBINS, the sober-minded Puritan girl was attracted by the gay carelessness of such a character. His vivacity and intelligence, his ardent temperament, his reckless courage, his songs and tales of wild adventure, captivated her, and under promise that "her people should be his people, her God his God," she married him. [43]

The disdain toward mixed marriages at the time is demonstrated by C. Alice Baker's account of these events:

> I must confess that I have always looked with less favor on two other marriages contracted that winter, that of Elizabeth Price to Andrew Stevens, the Indian, and that of Abigail Stebbins to James Denio, of whom all that we have hitherto known is that he was one of three Frenchmen then living in Deerfield. That these two girls, born of good Puritan stock, should have done this thing, and especially at a time when the very name of French and Indian was most hateful to the people of New England, has always shocked my sense of the fitness of things. Andrew Stevens, "the Indian," was killed at the sacking of the town His young wife, with James Denio and his bride, Abigail Stebbins, her father and mother and the rest of their children were captured. John Stebbins, his wife Dorothy and their two sons, John and Samuel, came back. Abigail and her husband, her sister Thankful, and her brothers, Ebenezer and Joseph, remained in Canada; so also did Elizabeth Price Stevens. The latter lived for a time with the Nuns of the Congregation, and having made formal abjuration of

the "Calvinistic heresy," was baptized on the 25th of April, 1705…[44]

Around the time of this wedding another unusual arrival, "Andrew Stevens, the Indian," married Elizabeth Price. The origin of Andrew Stevens, "the Indian", remains a mystery. It appears that he was an "Indian" by adoption and acculturation, not birth, and the characterization of him as "the Indian" suggests the degree to which some English still looked at Natives from the perspective of culture, not race. If he had been born a Native, his marriage to an Englishwoman by a New England minister would have been an unprecedented occurrence. If he was an Indian, he could have come from almost anywhere in the Northeast. Natives from all over New England, eastern New York, and Canada visited Deerfield. He was able to communicate with, and win the affections of, Elizabeth Price suggest a degree of fluency in English and a certain familiarity with English customs. A number of New England Natives possessed such knowledge. But his very English last name, combined with what would have been a very unusual proper name for a New Englander, might provide a clue to his origin. The combination of an English surname with a French-sounding proper name – Andrew or Andre – is a pattern often found among English captives rebaptized or merely renamed in Canada where French priests usually replace the Old Testament names of English captives with those of Christian saints. In the years after the Nine Years War, some English captured as children but now in their late teens or early twenties began to return after having lived in Native and French communities for several years. Stevens could have come to Deerfield with De Noyon, who had previously employed an English captive, Samuel York, as an intermediary with New York authorities.[45]

These stories of Andrew Stevens and Jacques de Noyon are more than romantic footnotes. They highlight the fact that even in times of war people moved between communities situated in antagonistic empires and different cultures. Such movements could be peaceful and unthreatening to the parties immediately involved. But other Frenchmen and Englishmen, and other Natives could see them as threatening. And for Andrew Stevens his relocation to Deerfield would prove fatal. Though not a direct cause of the Deerfield raid, the migration of the De Noyon and his companions was a symptom of the causes and calculations that were launching the expedition against the town.[46]

For my family this may have been a fortunate circumstance. As Baker put it,

"Perhaps his presence on that fateful night saved his wife's whole family from the tomahawk".[47] In fact, it also explains their relative safety on the march and the relative comfortable life they enjoyed while on captivity.

French/Indian Preparations

The Frenchmen included both regular army men and *coureurs de bois.* The Indians came from two groups: the Caughnawagas, or French Mohawks, and a larger group of Abenaki [perhaps my Indian ancestors], formally of Maine and now living – like the Caughnawaga – under French protection near Montréal.[48]

Many strange coincidences surround my branch of the Stebbins Family. A recent discovery shows that my branch of the family tree traces a direct bloodline to an Abenaki Indian, Heborah Theodota. As a result, I may have relatives on both sides of the upcoming battle.

Leaving Canada in the depths of winter, the party made its way south on snowshoes, walking atop frozen lakes and rivers, up the Sorel River to Lake Champlain, from the eastern side of Champlain up to the Winooski River, and eventually onto the upper Connecticut. As the French and Indians neared the end of their three-hundred-mile journey, they left a few of their party, plus sleds and provisions, some twenty-five miles above Deerfield. From there they moved overland toward the frontier village.[49]

Leading the war party was Sieur Hertel de Rouville, a regular French officer of the line. De Rouville's father, Francois Hertel, had been a great military leader, a hero in early New France particularly for leading a successful French and Indian raid on Salmon Falls, New Hampshire, in 1690. Now his son was about to launch a similar strike.[50]

As daylight waned on Monday, February 28, 1704, the French and Indians moved into position two miles north and across the river from Deerfield. From there they observed the activities of the town and planned their attack. As night fell, the villagers of Deerfield moved as usual into the fort. Roughly three-quarters of the townspeople had homes outside the palisade, but all took the precaution that night of sleeping within the ten- or twelve-foot high wall. With fortifications recently rebuilt and twenty garrison soldiers newly arrived, the town seemed well protected. Living conditions were extremely cramped and uncomfortable, though. With the addition of twenty soldiers, Deerfield now held 291 people, all packed into 10 or 12 houses inside the fort, plus the one fortified house of Captain Jonathan Wells just to the south. Still, it was better to be cramped and safe inside the fort than left outside to the mercies of the enemy. As the town went to bed, a watch regularly patrolled, protecting Deerfield's people as they slept.[51]

The guard of twenty men, allowed by the Council in May 1703, were now here quartered among the inhabitants, two of them in the house of the Minister. The winter wore away, even to the last day, and no enemy had been seen; the only alarm being the supernatural one, already noted. Mr. Williams, the pastor, did not share in the general feeling of security, and did not attempt to conceal his anxiety. He urged caution and vigilance, and above all, counseled the people to repentance of sin and to walking in the ways of righteous, that the wrath of God might be averted. He says:[52]

> I set apart a day of prayer, to ask of God, either to spare, and save us from the hands of our enemies, or prepare us to sanctify and honor him in what way soever he should come forth towards us * * * The places of Scripture from whence we were entertained were Gen. xxxii. 10. 11. *I am not worthy of the least of all the mercies, and of all the truth which thou hast shewed unto thy servants. Deliver me, I pray thee, from the hand of my brother, from the hand of something: for I fear him, lest he will come and smite me, and the mother with the children,* (in the fore noon.) And Gen. xxxii. 26, *And he said, let me go, for the day breaketh: And he said, I will not let thee go except thou bless me* (in the afternoon.) From which we were called upon to spread thick causes of fear, relating to ourselves, or families, before God; as also how it becomes us, with an undeniable importunity, to be following God, with earnest prayers for his blessing, in every condition. And it is very observable, how God ordered our prayers, in a peculiar manner, to be going up to him: to prepare us: with a right Christian spirit, to undergo, and endure suffering trials."[53]

Through the night, as the town slept, the French and Indians waited. And as they waited, what they observed gave them promise of aid. First, they saw that the heavy snows of winter, some three feet deep, still blanketed the area. That snow had made their travel to Deerfield difficult. Yet here it had drifted up against the palisade, and they now saw that they could easily mount the drifts and climb over the wall. Toward morning they saw something even more important: There was no watch.[54]

The invaders were provided with moccasins and snowshoes, and brought an extra supply for the use of captives.[55]

Provisions were brought along on sleds, some of which were drawn by dogs, and each man carried a pack upon his back. Their food becoming exhausted, the whole force was scantily supported on game killed by the Indian hunters. When De Rouville reached this vicinity, the French were half starved, almost a state of mutiny, and would doubtless have surrendered to the English at discretion had the attack on the town been unsuccessful.[56]

Settlers taken captive in 1703 from Deerfield are:

1703

Williams, Zebediah
Nims, John
    (Coleman 2:33)

Chapter 8

DEERFIELD: RAID OR MASSACRE?

Many accounts, some conflicting, have been offered about the attack on Deerfield, Feb. 29, 1704. The account by Haefelie & Sweeney, in this section appeared to be the best documented and most scholarly. I've included the text here in its entirety, unless otherwise noted.

Just before Dawn on February 29, 1704, the French and Indian army emerged from the fog of rumors and warnings and fell upon a sleeping Deerfield. The raiders had arrived in the area on the proceeding day. They then spent a fire-less night camped on Petty Plain just across the Deerfield River about two miles north of town. They would have been cold, hungry, and tired, but probably not on the verge of surrender, as some authors have wistfully suggested.[1]

Well before dawn the raiders crossed the Deerfield River and took up a position in the meadows north of the village. Scouts were dispatched to spy out the village. They returned and reported that a watch patrolled the stockade. The raiders waited. After a while, a second scouting party set forth. This party returned to report that all was now still and quiet. The watch apparently had fallen asleep. As they made their final preparations, Lieutenant Jean-Baptiste Hertel de Rouville probably called the *troopes* and militiamen together and, as he did on another occasion, exhorted 'all who had any quarrels with each other to be reconciled sincerely, and embrace.' They undoubtedly prayed. Native leaders likely delivered their own words of encouragement, and Christian Natives probably prayed as well. They set off toward the stockade. It was about 2 hours before Dawn.[2]

According to local Deerfield tradition, De Rouville had his men move forward in rushes to mimic gusts of wind. They would run forward, pause to listen, and run forward again. But moving rapidly on snowshoes across the snow that lay 3-feet deep on the open meadows would have been exhausting if not utterly impossible. They probably moved slowly and carefully, passing by a half-dozen abandoned houses that stood north of the stockade, until they reached the 10-foot palisade that ringed the score of dwellings houses in the center of the village. The thick blanket of snow that had pulled their feet and slowed their progress now aided their enterprise. Prevailing winds from the northwest had banked snow in drifts against the outside of the wall, eliminating its effectiveness as a barrier. Volunteers climbed the snowbanks, clambered over the top of the wall, and dropped down into the stockade, the deep snow breaking the fall. Once inside, they opened the north gate.[3]

Ideally, separate parties would have targeted individual houses inside the palisade and waited. Once everyone was in place, they would have struck simultaneously, forcing open the doors of the houses and bursting in upon still sleeping occupants. In the last war, such well-coordinated simultaneous assaults had overwhelmed the sleeping residents of almost every one of the houses. Escape had been impossible. Sixty residents died and 27 were captured. Casualties among the attackers had been only 2 killed and a couple wounded. At Salmon Falls, Hertel's father had successfully targeted and overwhelmed the hamlet's 3 fortified, garrison houses with coordinated attacks. In the process, his raiders killed 34 English and captured 54. Only 1 Frenchman had been mortally wounded during these assaults.[4]

At Deerfield something went wrong. Soon after entering the stockade the raiders lost the element of surprise and failed to position themselves as the raiders had at Schenectady and Salmon Falls. The Reverend John Williams later wrote that the watch had been unfaithful, allowing the French and Indians to enter the village undetected. Another report, however claimed that 'the watch shot off a gun and cried Arm' and thus gave a warning that a very few residents actually heard. Another possibility is that a surprised occupant might have fired the initial shot in response to a premature assault on one of the houses. It is unlikely that the raiders themselves fired such a shot. Their preferred weapons at this stage of an assault were axes, hatchets, clubs, and swords. For whatever reason, the raiders were not in place at each of the houses when the fighting began, nor had they succeeded in reaching the south gate to cut off one obvious avenue of escape.[5]

The great size and diversity of the raiding party was probably to blame. The variety of interests involved worked against the maintenance of the cohesion and discipline needed for a series of precisely coordinated assaults on the village's houses. One senses that there was a loss of control even before a single gun had been discharged.

The torrent of attackers divided into 3 streams as it passed through the gate (see Map 4). Some turned left and headed toward the houses lying east of the common. Others moved straight ahead and scattered among the small houses that had been erected on the common. Those moving the fastest proceeded to the houses on the west side of the common.[6]

Competition, rather than coordination characterized the assaults on individual dwellings as Native attackers raced toward likely houses to grab captives. A mixed party of over 20 Abenakis, Kahnawake Mohawks, and Pennacooks (including Wattanummon) attacked the home of Reverend John Williams during the initial onset. 'Violent endeavors to break open doors and windows with axes and hatchets' announced their arrival and awakened Williams. He called to 2 soldiers who slept upstairs and reached for his pistol. Cocking the pistol, he pointed it at the first Native who entered his room. Fortunately for Williams, it misfired; otherwise he would have been killed on the spot. Three Abenakis immediately seized Williams and disarmed him. The Native raiders – Williams makes no mention of Frenchman – moved through his house, ransacking it while rounding up his family. Wattanummon seized 10-year-old Stephen Williams. Mohawks took 7-year-old Eunice and 4-year-old Warham. Their older sister, Esther, probably became an Abenaki captive. Two of the young children, 6-year-old John and 6-week-old Jerusha, were killed as was Williams's female slave, Parthena. One of the soldiers, Lieutenant John Stoddard of Northampton, the commander of the garrison soldiers, escaped by jumping out an upstairs window. He ran to Hatfield to spread the alarm. The other soldier, probably Joseph Eastman of Hadley, was captured. So was Frank, the family's other slave. The captives were allowed to dress while they remained confined to their house. Residents of other homes suffered a similar fate.[7]

Where complete surprise was achieved, was at some of the houses just inside the north gate, whole families were taken with only the very young, those too small and weak to make the journey back to Canada, being killed. On the east side of the common, Kahnawake Mohawks and Iroquois of the Mountain overwhelmed occupants of the Carter and French houses without meeting serious resistance (see Map 4).

Fourteen members of these families were captured and 2 young children were killed outright. Only Samuel Carter managed to escape in the ensuing confusion. Nearby Native raiders also captured 5 of the 7 members of the Kellogg family. Hurons and Abenakis captured almost intact the families of David Hoyt Sr., John Stebbins,

Henry R. Stebbins Jr.

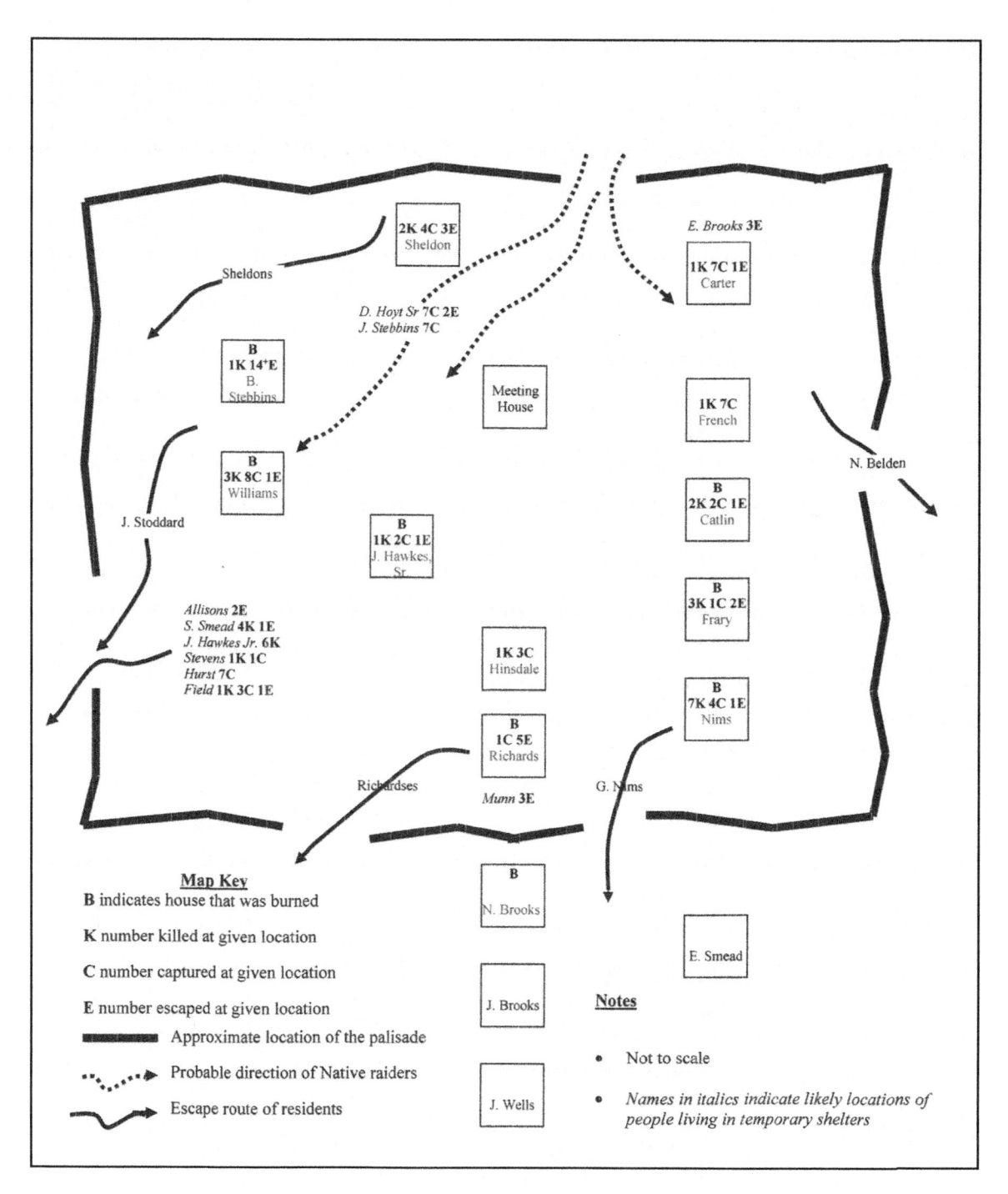

Map 5: Palisade
(Blackmer & Haefli/Sweeney)

and Simon Beamon. These families, whose homes lay outside of the palisade, were probably living near the north end of the stockade in small shelters that offered little protection against the raiders. All 4 members of the Warner family were also taken during the initial stages of the attack somewhere in the northern part of the stockade.[8]

These first, largely unopposed assaults had also bagged the trio of renegade Canadian fur traders. Most likely they were staying with the family of John Stebbins, Jacques de Noyon's father-in-law. De Noyon would have been immediately recognized by his former neighbor Ensign René Boucher and undoubtedly other French raiders, some of whom had been fur traders themselves. It must have been an awkward reunion that ended De Noyon's search for opportunity along the frontiers of New France and New England. He and 2 compatriots were now prisoners facing a long march back to Canada and an uncertain fate.[9]

Battle cries, terrified screams, and the occasional gunshot had aroused the rest of the village. Now the English began to fight back and adults were killed. Farther along the east side of the common, Hurons and Iroquois's of the Mountain, probably accompanied by some Abenakis, met with resistance at the homes of Catlin, Frary, Nims, and Mattoon families (see Map 4). The male heads of 3 of the households were killed: John Catlin Sr., Samson Frary, and Philip Mattoon. Only Godfrey Nims managed to escape. These families had had enough time to rouse and defend themselves, but not enough time to flee. Overall more members of these families were killed outright – 12 – then captured – 7. Resistance had probably provoked their assailants.[10]

These groups of Hurons, Iroquois, and Abenakis raiders, then crossed to the west side of the common (see Map 4). Here, in the southwestern corner of the stockade, residents had the most time to react. Some fled. Some try to hide. Most of the teacher John Richards's family got away by running through a nearby gate. John Allison and his wife 'escaped out the great gate meadow-ward [the west gate] and ran to Hatfield; she was frozen in her feet very much.' Allison's brother Thomas and the 84-year-old widowed mother somehow managed to avoid capture as well. John Field, John Hawkes Sr., Robert Price, and Samuel Smead also eluded the raiders, even though the remaining members of their families were taken prisoner or killed. It is possible that the women and children tried to hide while the men ran for help or to muster and fight in a body with the town's other militiamen. If this was their plan, it failed, tragically so for Samuel Smead's wife, mother, and 2 children, who died in hiding when their house was burned. Nearby, the entire family of John Hawkes Jr., along with Martin Smith, who lived with them, perished, either suffocated or incinerated when their house was burned above them.[11]

Given the confusion and the attackers' likely unfamiliarity with Deerfield, hiding could work. For over 3 hours, Ebenezer Brooks' family hid in a cellar of a temporary dwelling not far from the stockade's north gate. Sarah Kellogg initially hid under a washtub in the cellar of her house and then escaped the burning house almost naked. Near the south gate, Benjamin Munn and his family remained in a cellar that stood next to the home of his father-in-law, John Richards. The deep snow obscured this low structure, a temporary subterranean dwelling with a roof, and saved the Munn family. But elsewhere in the southern part of the village hiding was less successful. Most members of the Field, Hawks, Hurst, and Price families became prisoners. Relatively few, only 4, were killed outright in the southwestern part of the village, underscoring the fact that most of the attackers wanted prisoners and suggesting that those residents who did not flee did not put up much of a fight.[12]

Those who had been captives before did everything they could to avoid being captured again. Former captives such as Benoni Stebbins and Nathaniel Belding resisted or ran to avoid being taken prisoner again. Andrew

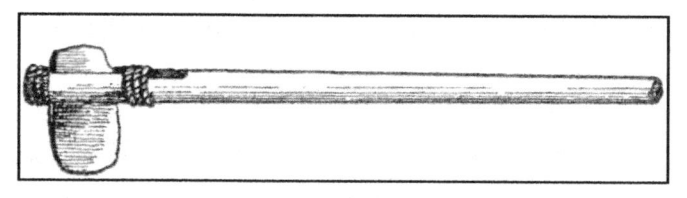

Indian Head Breaker
(Drake 107)

Stevens, 'the Indian,' was killed in the southwestern corner of the stockade. He may have died resisting capture, or he may have been recognized by former compatriots who responded violently to his new identity. Whatever his place of origin, he died in English village. Crossing cultural boundaries or resisting crossing could have terrible consequences. His English wife became and Indian captive and eventually married a Frenchman.[13]

The attackers met their strongest resistance in the northwest corner of the stockade. Here stood the houses of Ensign John Sheldon and Sergeant Benoni Stebbins. They had not been overwhelmed in the initial assaults. At the Sheldon house a barred front door [see picture below] proved to be a temporary deterrent. The Stebbins house, for some reason, had simply escaped the first wave of uncoordinated attacks. A belated attempt to enter the house was beaten back by its fully awakened defenders. Both houses were substantial frame structures with walls filled with nogging – loose, unfired bricks that served as insulation and added to the walls' ability to stop bullets.[14]

The door at the Sheldon house put up more of a fight than its occupants. John

Sheldon Jr., and his new wife, Hannah, attempted to escape by jumping out a second-story window. Hannah sprained her ankle when she landed and was unable to continue but encouraged John to flee to Hatfield to obtain help. He did, running all the way on feet barely covered with strips of cloth hastily torn from a blanket.

John Sheldon's House
In Deerfield, the most memorable relic to survive the French, Kanien'keha-ka (Mohawks), Abenaki, and Wenat-Huron attack in 1704 is the front door of the Ensign John Sheldon house, better known as the Old Indian House. John Sheldon (1658-c.1733) built his 42-by-21-house at the north end of the Common in 1699.
[also see photo of John Sheldon's house door]
(Flynt 17)

Another Hannah, the wife of John Sheldon Sr., was killed by a well-placed shot. At some point, her husband and a garrison soldier ran to the safety of Captain Jonathan Wells' garrison house, a fortified home that stood undisturbed several hundred yards south of the stockade (see Map 4). While all this was happening, the front door stoutly resisted the axes of its assailants. Eventually, Kahnawake Mohawks gained access by a less heroic back door. They brained two-year-old Mercy Sheldon just outside the now open front door and made prisoners of the three remaining Sheldon children. This house, along with the meetinghouse, became a holding area for those taking captives elsewhere.[15]

Next door, a larger contingent in the Stebbins house defiantly held out. In that house of Benoni Stebbins, 7 heroic men, seconded by their wives, for 3 hours kept at bay the combined force of French and Indians. Their children clinging to them in fright, unceasingly the women moulded bullets. Resolutely the men stood at their posts. The leaden hail beat steadily down upon the assailants. Fiercer and higher, rose the yells of the baffled foe.[16]

Up until this point, the French and Indians had met with very little resistance, taking prisoners at will and killing those who resisted. Now an opportunity for heroism called forth a competitive, at times reckless, quest for distinction, especially among the leaders. Parties of Hurons, Abenakis, and Frenchmen assaulted the house. The Hurons' great chief, an Abenaki captain – one of John Williams's three captors – and Ensign Francois-Marie Margane de Batilly received mortal wounds leading charges. Even De Rouville received a wound, though it is not certain exactly when and where he was shot. Several of their men perished in an unsuccessful effort to fire the house. Frustrated, the attackers tried negotiating with the defenders, offering them quarter if they lay down their arms. They refused. Benoni Stebbins did not want to be captive again. After these fruitless efforts to carry the house by force, fire, and persuasion, the raiders retired to more protected positions. Safe inside the neighboring Sheldon house and the meetinghouse, they fired at the Stebbins house. At one point it appeared as though the entire French and Native force ringed the house and poured in shots.[17]

With a seemingly unlimited supply of powder and shot, the house's occupants kept up a steady fired that held their assailants at bay for over two-and-a-half hours. The house had heavy doors and slots for shooting. Seven men, including Benoni Stebbins, David Hoyt Jr., Joseph Catlin, Benjamin Church, and a 24-year-old garrison soldier from Hadley, and three others, 4 or 5 women, and uncertain number of children managed to beat back scores of attackers. Quite likely some of them were using fowling pieces or large bore muskets charged with small shot that effectively turned their weapons into shotguns. One did not have to be a marksman: the scatter from a single discharge of a gun with small shot could have hit a half-dozen men. Some fired

The Dead 1704

40 rounds. Frenchman and Natives fired back, eventually killing Benoni Stebbins and wounding Mary Hoyt and one of the garrison soldiers, probably Church.[18] Benoni Stebbins, after fighting for hours like a tiger at bay, lay dead in his house.[19] Benoni died defending his home and was buried in a common grave with the other dead Deerfield defenders.

At 8 o'clock the main body of the enemy had withdrawn. Friendly horsemen from neighboring towns had newly arrived could see the remnant enemy forces were still besieging Benoni's house.[20] Outside the house a Huron chief had received a mortal wound, he was one of John Williams's 3 captors.[21]

Elsewhere in the village, Frenchman and Natives set about the work of despoiling Deerfield. They rounded up prisoners and ransacked houses. The captives they herded together in the meetinghouse and the Sheldon House. At some point they started burning houses, beginning with those toward the south end of the stockade and gradually working their way north. The also killed all the cattle, hogs, and sheep they could find, "sacking and wasting all that came before them." All this was part of a spoiling raid designed to terrify and materially damage the enemy. Some Abenakis and the Mohawks began moving their prisoners out the north gate. They headed toward the previous night's camp on Petty Plain. Along the way they looted the 6 houses that lay north of the stockade and burned 4 of them.[22]

Now was the most dangerous time for the attackers. Raiding parties were at their most vulnerable as they withdrew. Tired and drained by battle, slowed and distracted by captives, and loaded down with plunder, they could blunder into an ambush or be run down by determined pursuers. Most of the deaths on the Schenectady and Salmon Falls raids and a later Haverhill raid occurred while the Raiders were withdrawing or trekking back to Canada. Lacking cohesion and discipline since they had first entered the north gate, the Deerfield raiding party was especially vulnerable. During the ensuing three to three-and-a-half hours, they had been badly shot up.[23]

Sometime after the withdrawal had begun, a relief party of English militiamen entered the stockade's south gate. The glow of fires had alerted residents of towns to the south. Thirty to forty men had ridden from Hatfield and Hadley to Deerfield. Still on horseback, they entered the palisade through the south gate. Most of the raiders had probably left, but some remained, looting and shooting at the Stebbins house. Preoccupied with plunder and arson, the raiders still inside the stockade were probably slow to react to the unexpected challenge. Some Natives were apparently more concerned with making a getaway with their captives. According to a French source, "the French, with the Lorettans and Abnaquis alone sustained and repelled the onset, the other savages having been shamefully put to flight." It must've been a wild and confused battle.[24]

The English militiamen persisted, gaining strength as the men of Deerfield joined them. At some point men from Captain Jonathan Wells' garrison house entered the fray. This strong point lying south of the palisade had provided refuge for some of those fortunate enough to have escaped death or capture within the stockade. It also contained part of the village's contingent of garrison soldiers. The reinforced militiamen eventually drove out the remaining raiders. As the English militiamen pushed forward, the raiders fled, dropping their plunder as they ran. The rescuers raised the siege of the Stebbins house and forestalling the burning of the stockade's northernmost houses. This timely action spared Ebenezer Brooks and his family, who were hiding in a temporary shelter located somewhere near the northern end of the stockade.[25]

Encouraged by the success and undoubtedly enraged by the death and destruction all around them, the militiamen pushed on. Two defenders of the Stebbins house, David Hoyt Jr., and Joseph Catlin, joined the party. As a relief party passed through the north gate and headed down the street for the meadows, it numbered close to sixty men. Running headlong and undisciplined, the mostly youthful militiamen [probably Benjamin Stebbins, who at age 12, would have wanted revenge for his father's [Benoni] death, hotly burning in his heart] pursued the retiring raiders. They threw off hats, coats, jackets, and accoutrements in an effort to close the gap between themselves and the last of the fleeing attackers. One of the pursuers, a Deerfield resident named John Smead, killed one Native, who was promptly scalped. He then wounded another. As a contemporary author admitted, such marksmanship was 'a rare thing amongst us.' But without snowshoes, the English floundered in the deep snow, became separated, and stood exposed in the open meadows.[26]

De Rouville now faced a pitched battle. Given the experiences of previous raiding parties, he may well have anticipated this contingency. Certainly, the shots fired by the English relief party as it charged into the village and then on to the north meadows would have alerted him to the danger he now faced. Just as his father had at Salmon Falls, he rallied his Canadians and laid an ambush. A mile or a mile and half from the village, he posted thirty of his men along 'a River Bank'.[27]

Heedless of their danger the English rushed forward. They ran across the meadow, 'impudently' advancing 'too far' in the opinion of a contemporary observer. Sensing danger, Captain Jonathan Wells called a retreat. His men ignored him. On command,

The Dead 1704

Captive or Burn		Slain	Alive at Home	Estate lost
John Stebbins	7: himself, wife & 5 children	0	0	100 house burnt & Estate in it
Benoni Stebbins		1: himself	6: Wife & 5 children	+300 house & all goods, barn & cattle burnt

100 & +300 represents the value of houses, barns, etc., in English pounds
(Greenlee 106 & 114)

Hertel's men 'rose up' and fired a volley into the English. The shock caused English 'to give back.' The relatively rested Canadians joined by some of the Natives move forward. The pursuers became the pursued. Much later, English survivors of the Meadows Fight would claim that they fell back cautiously, maintaining their composure, while 'facing [about] and firing, so that those who first failed might be defended.' But in the immediate aftermath, participants admitted, 'we were overpowered & necessitated to run to the fort & in our flight, nine of the company were slain & some others wounded.' The number of dead and wounded suggests a breakdown of discipline and flight.[28]

The raiders do not appear to of press their advantage. With their superior numbers and greater mobility (because of snowshoes), they could have run down and cut off most of the retreating English. But neither the Natives nor the Frenchman needlessly exposed themselves. Much safer, less exhausting, and only slightly less effective was their tactic of advancing cautiously and maintaining their distance. Among the nine Englishmen they killed were Catlin and Hoyt. [No doubt carelessly seeking revenge while filled with adrenaline.] They wounded several others and captured John Marsh, a militiaman from Hatfield. But they have their losses too, 5 killed and others wounded. The English counterattack had practically doubled the raiders' losses. Fighting ended when the English militiamen regained the protection of the stockade.[29]

Reinforcements from the Massachusetts towns below Deerfield continued to come in during the day. As the alarm traveled south, militiamen from Northampton and the Springfield area mounted and rode north. By midnight almost 80 men had gathered in Deerfield. There were those who favored launching an immediate rescue operation. In the past, pursuits had on occasion, freed captives. Others objected that without snowshoes, they would be forced to follow directly in the retreating raiders' path and thus be open to ambush and flank attacks by the more mobile enemy. The beating that the English had received in the Meadows Fight undoubtably cooled the ardor of some. The raiders still had a decided advantage in numbers. Finally, some 'were much concerned for the Captives, Mr. Williams' family especially, whome the Enemy would kill, if we come on.'[30]

By two o'clock the next day, March 1, militiamen started arriving from the Connecticut towns around Hartford. As night fell again, there were about 250 men in Deerfield, a number almost equal to that of the raiders. They debated their course of action. The objections raised the day before were repeated: the lack of snowshoes, the risk to the captives, and the danger to the would-be rescuers. The weather now raised another objection: it grew warmer and began to rain. The deep snow turned into a slushy quagmire that even snowshoes could have traversed only with difficulty. Pursuit on horses would've been difficult as well and would have increased the likelihood of rushing headlong into an ambush. After assigning some of their numbers to form a garrison to protect what remained of the devastated village, the bulk of the militiamen headed for home.[31]

Those men who stayed assisted grief-stricken residents in the grim task of counting and burying the dead. The destruction from fire made identifying, and in some cases even finding bodies difficult. Colonel Samuel Partridge composed a detailed tally of losses and send it on to Governor Fitz-John Winthrop of Connecticut. Allowing for later adjustments, Partridge's accounting revealed that 41 had died in town: 38 residents and 3 garrison soldiers. Only 2 were definitely known to have died of gunshot wounds in the village; at least 15 had been consumed by fire. Edge weapons or clubs probably killed most of the remainder. Another 9 had been killed in the Meadows Fight: 7 from the towns below and 2 Deerfield residents. Others, it is not clear how many, had been wounded.[32]

Macqua Chief
(Drake 253)

The overall pattern of casualties reflects primarily choices made by adult males – Native, French, and English – in the heat of battle. A high proportion of those slain were very young children, who had very little value as captives and would not have been strong enough anyway to make the grueling trek back to Canada. Though adult men and women had died in about equal numbers, more men than women had escaped capture. At least 2 garrison soldiers and 8 other men had fled and thus avoided the captivity or death that befell a majority of their family members. Some had run for help; some had apparently just run. One hundred and eleven had been captured and removed from the village by the raiders. A majority of the captives were women and older children, who were probably viewed as possible adoptees into Native communities. One of the garrison soldiers, John Bridgeman, escaped during the Meadows Fight, but another militiaman, John Marsh, had been captured during the fight.[33]

In addition to taking captives and lives, the raiders had sought to devastate the village and make it unlivable. Burning the houses and killing livestock had been purposeful, not just wanton destruction. Twelve houses inside and 5 outside of the stockade had been destroyed. Barns had also been torched and in them were lost livestock, tools, and provisions. Only 9 houses remained standing within the stockade; to the north of the stockade 2 houses belonging to the Hoyts had apparently escaped destruction; another 13 still stood intact and undisturbed along the street south of the stockade. Partridge's Table of Losses makes clear that the 13 families living in these houses had escaped unmolested by the attackers. They undoubtedly had the resistance at the Stebbins house and the breakdown of discipline and direction among the raiders to thank for their remarkable delivery.[34]

Casualties among the raiders had also been heavier than one would expect for a battle later characterized as a massacre. The French especially had been hurt. Twenty-two had been wounded, among them De Rouville, one of his brothers, Boucher, Legardeur, and Margane, who was mortally wounded. Two other Frenchman, 5 "Maquas" [i.e., Mohawks, Hurons and Iroquois of the Mountain] and 3 "Indians" [i.e., Abenakis and Pennacooks] had been killed. It is also apparent the some of the wounded subsequently died during the return march. After the battle the English appear to have stripped about 8 corpses. Other English sources claim that 30 to 50 of the raiders had died, and John Williams later insisted that 'the French always endeavor to conceal the number of their slain.' But the English claims are too high to be credible. The English militiamen were not good enough shots to have killed that many French and Indians outright. The admiration for John Smead's marksmanship in the Meadows Fight is evidence of its rarity. Four years later during a fiercely contested attack on Haverhill, Massachusetts, 160 French and Indian raiders faced a force that included

30 garrison soldiers and then retreated into an ambush laid by a relief party of another 60 English militiamen, but only 7 Frenchman and 3 Indians were killed, 18 wounded, and 1 captured. Still, compared with the relatively light losses occurred in other raids against New England, the Deerfield raid was the costliest for the French and their Native allies.[35]

The French exaggerated their success at Deerfield. In reports and memorials to officials in France, Governor Vaudreuil and the Hertels sought to enhance the stature of their achievement. The size of the raiding party shrank to 200 while the stockaded village of Deerfield became 'fort guerifil where there were a hundred-and twenty-seven armed men.' Additionally, De Rouville and 30 men had to fight off a relief party of 'more than one hundred men.' The number of English-dead almost tripled to 150 and the number of captives inflated to 170. Claude de Ramezay, the governor of Montréal and Philippe de Vaudreuil's rival and critic, appears to have precisely reported the numbers involved and downplayed the achievement. He dismissively characterized Deerfield as 'a small village of about forty homesteads.' Later, Charles Legardeur would also correctly characterize Deerfield as a 'small village.'[36]

Despite the high proportion of casualties, the assault was a clear-cut tactical victory that furthered the strategic goals of Governor Vaudreuil. By deploying fewer than 50 Frenchman, the governor had rallied Native support and spread fear throughout New England. The commitment of these men demonstrated French willingness and ability to stand by their Native allies, and helped ensure that these allies would carry the war to the English. After such a bloody raid it became harder for Natives to make peace with the English. In addition, Native allies gained valuable captives to adopt, or ransom, alleviating some of the economic problems caused by the collapse of the beaver trade. Even before the Deerfield raiders had returned, Vandreuil had resolved to 'send forth another campaign.'[37]

In response, the New England colonies had to mobilize and commit hundreds of militiamen to frontier defense and expand expend thousands of pounds to protect and reassure the fearful residents of exposed towns. In the Connecticut valley, Samuel Partridge found that 'our people are so tranceported with the late stroak at Derefd that I can hardly pacifie them without men to garrison our towns.' By summer 1704, Massachusetts had nineteen hundred men under arms. Most of these men were kept in garrisons along a 200-mile frontier that stretched from Deerfield in the west to Wells, Maine, in the east. Dispersal and employment of so many men in passive and expensive frontier defenses rather than offensive of operations indirectly protected

Native and French communities and created political problems for the governments of the English colonies. The alternative of abandoning towns and drawing in the English colonies' frontiers would have entailed costs as well and created its own problems. The assault on Deerfield gave the strategic initiative in the war to the French.[38]

Chapter 9

ADDITIONAL NOTES ON THE BATTLE

Watchman Controversy

The reasons that Deerfield was apparently caught sleeping, was presented by Sheldon[1] in the following comment:

> The several statements, already given, referring to the sentinel appointed to watch the town, and warn the sleeping inhabitants in case of danger, appear quite contradictory. But a tradition told me by Mrs. Sylvia Munn, when in her 88th year, may be interpreted to reconcile them all. She said she had 'always heard,' that while on his beat, towards morning, the wearied watchmen heard from one of the houses, the soft voice of a woman, singing a lullaby to a sick child; that he stopped, and leaning against the window of the room where the child lay, listened to the soothing tones of the singer until he fell asleep. If this story be true, he was doubtless rudely aroused from his criminal slumber by the noise of the attack, and was the man referred to in the Winthrop paper as 'ye watch who shot off a gun & cryed Arm, wch verry few heard.' The alarm came too late, and they soon 'took ye watch captive.'

Henry R. Stebbins Jr.

Fatal Wounding of the Frenchman

The following letter[2] from a Catlin relative tells an authentic story from the Catlin family tradition that concerns the wounding of a Frenchman in the attack on the Benoni Stebbins house:

Coleraine Nov. 1, 1875

Mr. Sheldon:

DEAR SIR, – John Catlin, the captive, was born in the 50th year of his mother's age, and never have slept out of his father's house till the age of 16, when he was taken captive, and went to Canada in company with the sister. His sister was very delicate, never had endured any hardship, but performed the journey so well that the Indians would give her something to carry; she would carry it a little way, and throw it back as far as she could throw it. He (John) used to tremble for fear they would kill his sister, but they would laugh, and go back and get it. They acted as though they thought she was a great lady. The captives suffered from hunger, but she had plenty, and gave some to her brother. What her name was or what became of her I cannot tell. [Ruth, and she was redeemed.] He (John) was given to a French Jesuit. The Jesuit tried to persuade him to become a Catholic, but when he found he could not, told him he might go home when he had an opportunity; and when an opportunity presented, furnished him what he needed for the journey, and give him some money when he parted with him. He was with him two years.

His father and uncle [brother Jonathan?] were killed in the house; he took his father's gun, and his uncles powder horn, and was going to use them when the Indians took him. The captives were taken to the house, (I do not know what house) and a Frenchman was brought in and laid on the floor; he was in great distress, and called for water, Mrs. Catlin fed him with water. Someone said to her "how can you do that for your enemy?" She replied, "If thine enemy hunger, feed him; if he thirst, give him water to drink." The Frenchman [Probably De Rouville's brother] was taken and carried away, and the captives marched off. Mrs. Catlin was left. After they were all gone, a little boy came that was hid in the house. Mrs. Catlin said to the boy, "go run and hide." The boy said, "Mrs. Catlin, why don't you go and hide?" She said, "I am a captive; it is not my duty to hide, but you have not been taken, and it is your duty to hide." Who this boy was, I do not know? Some thought the kindest showed to the Frenchman was the reason of Mrs. Catlin's being left.

Lucy D Shearer

Sheldon House's Door

Below, Sheldon[3] chronicles the story of the famous door and John Sheldon's escape to seek help from Hatfield:

> The stout door of Ensign John Sheldon's house resisted the efforts to break it down. It was cut partly through with axes, and bullets fired through the place at random, one of which killed Mrs. Sheldon as she was sitting on a bed in the east room. Entrance was finally affected at the back door, which, according to a family tradition, was left open by a lad who sought safety in flight. Most of the family were captured. Probably the Ensign was not at home. His son, the newly married John, with his wife jumped from the east chamber window [and was captured]. The tradition says also that the 2 years old Mercy was taken to the front door and her brains dashed out on the door-stone: and further, that the house, being the largest in the town,

was reserved as a depot for captives. Here, then, was the place where Mrs. Catlin relieved the wounded French lieutenant, and secured her own freedom by her practical Christianity. It was certainly used as a cover and point of attack on the Stebbins house. It was set on fire, when the last marauders were driven away, but it was saved, and stood until 1849 – the widely known "Old Indian House." The scarred and battered door, supported by the original door posts and flanked by great oaken brackets from the front of the house, is now a center of attraction at Memorial Hall.

John Sheldon's House Door
From a postcard in the Memorial Hall Museum Pocumtuck Valley Memorial Association Deerfield, Massachusetts

Benoni Stebbins House

[The following emphasis *PROUDLY* placed in italics, by Henry R. Stebbins Jr.]

The Dead 1704

The group of heroes in this otherwise sad tale fought from a house owned by Sgt. Benoni Stebbins, my great (x6) granduncle. As Sheldon[4] so very eloquently wrote:

> "In all the wars of New England, there is not a more gallant act recorded than this defense of an unfortified house, by seven men and a few women, for three hours, against, not only the fury and wiles of an unorganized horde of savages, but also a large force of French soldiers, under officers of the line trained in the wars of France."

> "The Benoni Stebbins house, so heroically preserved from the fury and fagots of the enemy, sad to relate, accidentally took fire and was burned after the valiant garrison had joined the knights of the rescue in the pursuit of the assailants."

Lincoln Wells Homestead stands where once *"the dwelling of Benoni Stebbins, forever to be venerated as the spot where he, and six other brave men, nobly aided by the women, 'stood stoutly to your arms... With more than ordinary courage,* says an eyewitness of that dreadful day."[5]

The only resistance that the marauders seem to have met with came from the house of Benoni Stebbins, just mentioned, in which seven brave men and a few courageous women successfully defended themselves during all the time that the carnage raged fiercest around them. Mr. Williams himself an eyewitness of the determined efforts to capture this house, saw the same Indian whom he had failed to shoot shortly before, shot dead from it. *Although the gallant Stebbins had fallen, and two of his brave companions were badly wounded, in spite of coaxing, promises, or threats, to all of which the heroic defenders turned a deaf ear, this one house continued to stand firm as a rock in the midst of the storm of fire and blood surging around it long after the enemy were masters of the rest of the village.*[6]

My pistol missing fire was an occasion of my life's being preserved; since which I have also found it profitable to be crossed in my own will. *The judgment of God did not long slumber against 1 of the 3 which took me, who was a captain, for by sunrising he received a mortal shot from my next neighbor's house; who opposed so great a number of French and Indians as 300, and yet there were no more than 7 men in an un-garrisoned house.*[7]

Chapter 10

FORCE MARCHED INTO CAPTIVITY

Considerations

After the fight, it wasn't over for the Deerfield captives. It was March, the dead of winter, on a wooded/hilly landscape covered by deep snow and no shelter.

The sack of Deerfield had been a tremendous victory for the French and Indian Raiders, but the march north threatened to deny the allies of the fruits of their victory. John-Baptiste Hertel de Rouville, the nominal leader of the expedition, calculated victory in terms of property destroyed and enemy killed. Now his main goal was to get back quickly and safely. But for most of the 200-plus Native warriors without whom that victory would have been impossible, the fruits of victory were marching alongside them: 109 English captives. Preserving these fruits of victory involve a series of challenging negotiations on the march back to Canada and then in New France. Warriors had to cope with difficult winter weather, the weak and fearful, yet stubborn, English captives, and the occasionally contradictory demands of their mourning – war traditions and new Christian values. The march back to Canada exposed the complexity of the Natives' relationship to the English, the French, and Christianity.

Most of the warriors had joined expedition to take captives, and the Deerfield raid had been something of a bonanza in this respect. The size of the expedition and the achievement of surprise had allowed the warriors to gather as many captives as they could get their hands on. There was roughly 1 captive for every 3 raiders – an unusually high proportion for raiding parties. So many warriors had captives, or a share in a captive, that those who did not began to grumble. But capturing English colonists was one thing. Getting them back alive was another. As the party moved

109

north, a brutal weeding out process took place. At most, only 89 of the Deerfield captives eventually reached Canada. Most of those who died on the march were adult women – many of whom were weakened by childbirth and pregnancy – and very young children. Few adult males died, and under very different circumstances from the rest. In other words, the retreat was something of a disappointment for those men motivated by the customs of the mourning war. The captives they killed were exactly the sort they preferred to adopt into their communities.[2]

The English pursuit into the meadows had thrown the raiders into a state of confusion in which they lost control of some of their captives. One of the captured garrison soldiers, John Bridgman, had escaped during the fighting. Another captive, 3-year-old Marah Carter, had been killed, probably because she slowed down her fleeing master. During the night, as the army camped on the northern shore of the Deerfield River, 23-year-old Joseph Alexander escaped, suggesting disorder among the attackers.[3]

The killing of John Williams's slave Frank is further evidence of a breakdown in discipline and hints at the sometime tense relationship between African-Americans and Native Americans in the Northeast. On the evening of February 29, some of the raiders consumed liquor that they had plundered in Deerfield, and 'in their drunken fit' killed Frank. He was the only adult male killed outright on the march to Canada.[4]

De Rouville tried to restore a degree of order and discipline. A rear guard was detailed to protect the column during the coming day's march. He ordered John Williams 'to tell the English that, if any more made their escape, they would burn the rest of the captives.' It was a real threat. Only a few years before, Abenakis in Maine had recaptured two English captives who had tried to escape and tortured them to death as an example to the others. As the brother of one of the victims later recalled, their 'noses and ears were cut off and they [were] made to eat them, after which they were burned to death at the stake. The Indians at the same time declar[ed] that they would serve all deserters in the same manner.' Kahnawake Mohawks and Iroquois of the Mountain also tortured and burned escapees they recaptured. With this fate in mind, no more Deerfield captives tried to escape on the march north.[5]

As the English militiamen huddled in the village realized, and attempted rescue represented a serious threat to the captives' lives. Stephen Williams later recalled that the raiders told the captives that 'if the English pursued them, they would kill us, but if otherwise they would not.' French and Native raiders preferred to kill the captives rather than lose them to rescuers. Only four months later, in May 1704, a party of about 20 French and 50 Pennacooks successfully attacked Pascommuck, and outlying hamlet of Northampton. They captured 37 people but were hotly pursued by company of horsemen from Northampton. As the English troopers drew near, the French and Pennacooks knocked 'all the Captives in the head save 5 or 6.' Then, less encumbered by captives, they fought off their pursuers and escaped with 3 of the captives. Twenty prisoners, mostly adult men and young children, died. The decision not to pursue the Deerfield captives probably averted a real massacre.[6]

As a rule, French officers familiar with the culture of their Native allies avoided interjecting themselves into such disputes and let Natives dispose of captives as they deem fit. Experienced Canadian officers, such as Hertel de Rouville, knew that their superiors wanted English towns destroyed and depopulated. To achieve this goal on the New England frontier they needed the help of Native allies in Canada, who now largely fought parallel wars to capture people rather than towns. Especially on campaigns where most of the raiders were Indians, not French, officers had no way of enforcing European customs regarding the treatment of prisoners. When French officers tried to give English prisoners the sort of treatment Europeans expected, as Pierre Le Moyne de Iberville had at Pemaquid in 1696, and as Marquis de Montcalm would during the Seven Years War, they risk alienating their Native allies. The Hertels did not because they usually let their Native allies control the captives taken in their joint raids. At Deerfield, De Rouville had made something of an exception, because of the presence of the 3 Frenchmen. The French raiders clearly retained control of Jacques de Noyon, his wife, and the 2 other *coureurs de bois*. Some members of the Stebbins family, De Noyon's in-laws, and at least 2 members of the Burt family also apparently stayed in French custody the entire way back to Canada. In all at least 10 captives turned up in the home villages of French raiders – Boucherville, Chambly, and Varennes – sometime in mid-April without any sign of having passed through the hands of the Native captors.[7]

Again, that roguish French fur trader had inadvertently affected the course of Stebbins history by enabling John's family to safely trek up to the relatively cozy comfort of a town in Quebec in the company of the French.

Route of the Captives

The night of February 29th, the party camped at Greenfield Meadows, in the swamp east of the old Nims house. The next day they crossed Green River at the foot of Leyden hills, where the monument to Mrs. Eunice Williams marks the spot where she was killed. Thence up the hill in the old Indian path, still to be seen, northeasterly through Leyden, Bernardston, Vernon to the mouth of West river in Brattleboro, where they had left their heavy baggage, dogs, sledges, &c., arriving there, March 2nd. Thence up the Connecticut river on the ice. Sunday, March 5th, the army was at the mouth of Williams River, where Mr. Williams preached to the captives, who sang "one of Zion's Songs" to the Indians at their request. The river got its name from this occurrence. March 6th continuing on the river, they reached the mouth of White river March 8th. Here the party was broken up, the larger part going up White river. The St. Francis, or Abenaki Indians with Stephen Williams, David Hoyt, Jacob Hickson, and perhaps others, continued up the Connecticut. After months of wandering, this party struck across to French river, and went down that to Lake Champlain, down the lake, and the Sorel arriving at Chambly in August, and thence to the Indian fort at St. Francis.[8]

"The Caghnawagna Indians, with whom was Mr. Williams, went over the Green Mountains, and struck French river about March 18th. They reach the Sorel, March 29th, and Chambly, April 1st, being a little over a month on the march."[9]

The pathetic story of the dreadful March to Canada 'at least 300 miles,' and 'the snow up to the knees,' by this miserable band of men, women and children, as told by Mr. Williams in the 'Redeemed Captive,' is accessible to all, and is as familiar as household words to every student of New England history.[10]

Care of the Captives

The care of prisoners became a burden, and in 1704 Vaudreuil wrote to Versailles repeating Frontenac's request. He says: 'A large number of English prisoners whom we are obliged to clothe and feed, some being persons of consideration, whom we have bought from the Indians give us great expense,' and he hopes His Majesty will make the concession for which they beg.[11]

That a formal application was made two years later is shown by a ragged scrap of discolored paper which a book-lover of Québec treasured for its signatures of Vaudreuil and Raudot. It has the names of others [including Therese Steben].[12]

The Dead 1704

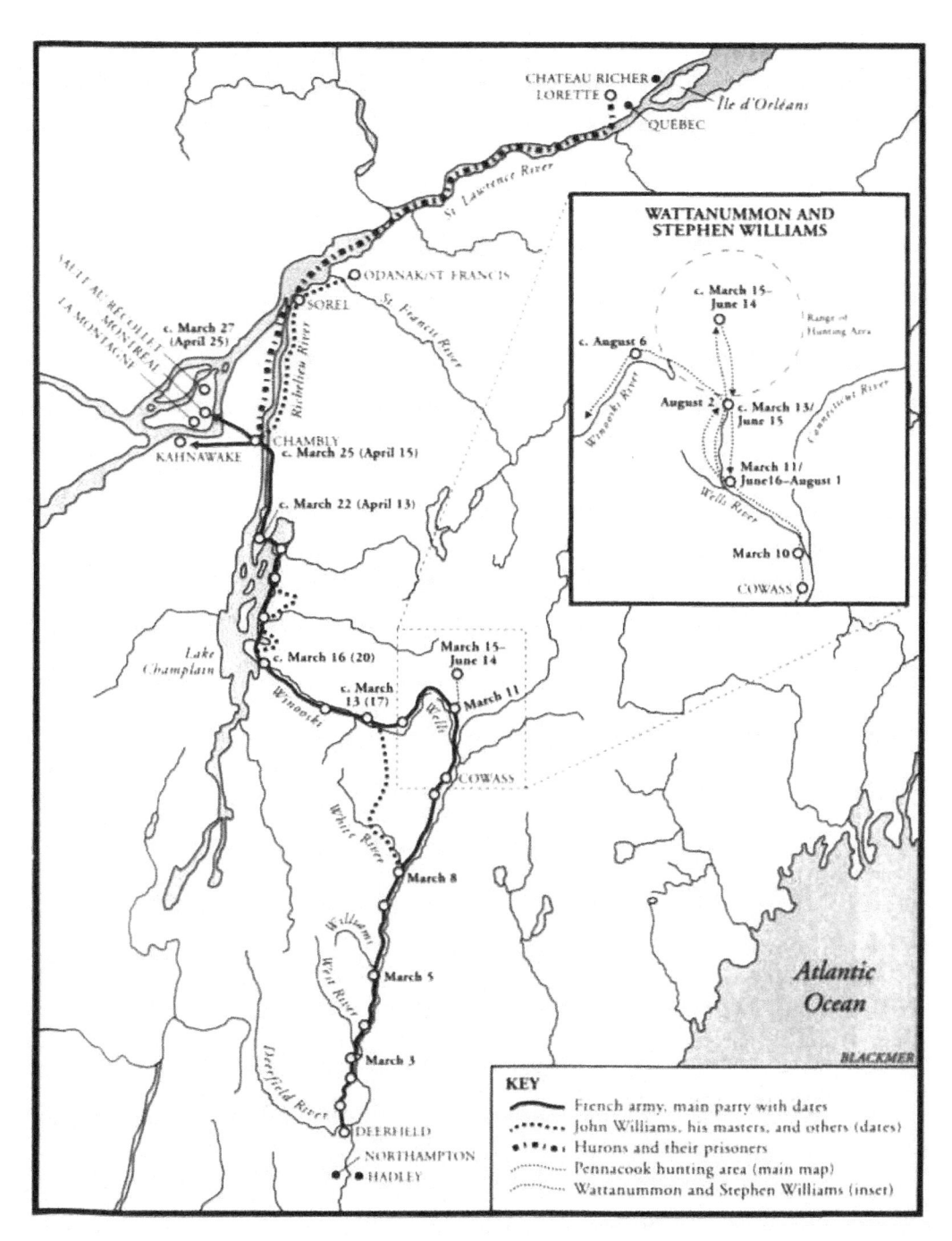

Map 6: Captive's Route
(Haefeli & Sweeney 119)

Henry R. Stebbins Jr.

In the month of May, 1710, Louis, 14th of his name, gave at Versailles in the grandest manner his gracious permission to these and other boys and girls, men and women, to live and die in New France or elsewhere in his possessions.[13]

'Louis, by the grace of God, King of France and Navarre, to all present and to come, greeting:

Our well beloved… [the list given includes: Jacques Charles Stebbens; Marguerite Stebbins, married to Jean des Noyons, sergeant, with children; Louise Therese Stebbens]… all professing the catholic, apostolic and roman religion, have shown us that they have been established several years in New France and desiring to end their days as our subjects, they have very humbly suplicated us to grant these Letters which facilitate in every way possible their residence in the "country of Canada and New France, ' they yielding obedience to us.[14]

The above named are to have -

'all the rights, privileges and immunities enjoyed by our born subjects, and well as the same rights to hold and dispose of property, real and personal,'

but: –

'They cannot leave the country without our express and written permission, nor can they either transmit information nor be employed as go-betweens with foreigners on pain of forfeiting these rights.'

Given at Versailles May, 1710.

Signed & 'sealed with the great seal with green wax on ribbons of red and green silk.'[15]

Chapter 11

POST BATTLE FALLOUT

Compensation for Scalps, Plunder and Losses

The practice of 'scalping' was brought to New England and was taught to the Indians before 1620 by the Dutch.[1] As with the Indians, the English settlers were involved in the practice of 'scalping'. For the English it was a sure way of providing proof for securing the bounty often given for scalps. The loss of a scalp was a sure sign for the demise of its former owner.[2] quotes the General Assembly in its June 8th, 1704 in the following resolution:

> That the Summ of five Pounds be paid to each of the widows of those Slain and mentioned in the List annexed, being four in number. [Sergt. Boltwood, Joseph Catlin, David Hoyt and Sergt. Waite].
>
> And altho but one Scalp of Indians slain by them is Recovered, yet for their Encouragem^t, that the sum of Sixty Pounds be allowed and Paid to the Petitioner whose names are contained in s^d list annexed as serving, as Scalp money, to be equally Divided amongst them. Together with all Plunder whereof they give account.

A second action by the Assembly that day dealt with articles of clothing lost by the rescuers in the Meadow Fight.[3]

The third action[4] of the Assembly that day involved compensation for the plunder that was captured. The portion related to the Stebbins family is included here:

> The list, includes Benia[n] stebing on[e] pistill for 10 shillings, plus the weapons, etc. seized in the battle by the other combatants. The powder horn carried by Ebenezer Searls on this occasion is among the relics in Memorial Hall.

In 1736, when the General Court was granting land on the slightest- provocation, Jonathan Wells and 53 others asked for a township in consideration of being in the Meadow Fight, and received a grant of 11,037 acres, joining Hatfield on the west.[5]

Papers in the Massachusetts Archives show that three men were wounded in the Meadow Fight, one, a prisoner, in mere wantonness. We learn that John Snead, after doing a heroic service, received a bullet in his thigh. Thomas Wells, Joseph Cleesson and John Arms certified that John Smead was in the fight and carried the bullet to his death, in 1720. In a petition to the General Court, May, 1743, his son John says of him:[6]

> By the blessing of Providence on his Endeavors, 'tis thot he did as much or more Spoil on the Enemy as any man there, * * * slaying two of the Indian Enemy, which, it is likely, is more than any other person did, & which Experience shows, has been a rare thing amongst us.

The following certificate accompanied this petition:

> I was in Dearfield Meadow fight, * * * and I see the said Smead kill an indian, & some of the souldiers tock off this Indian's scalp & secured it, & I see the said John Smead shoot at another Indian, which he gave a mortal wound, y[e] Indian died in a short time at the place where he received y[e] wound, or very near the place.
>
> Ebenezer Warner

Two hundred acres of land at Poquoig were granted the petitioner, Jan. 14th, 1743.[7] Samuel Church of Hadley, in a petition for aid, May, 1705, says:

> 'Having Rec[d] a Wound in my Arme in y[e] fight at Derefield feb[r] 29 1703 – 4 In the healeing of s[d] Wound I was disabled for to work & Labor for the space or tyme of twelve weeks & am weak and my Arm still Humbly Petition &c &c***it having been a great hinderence to me & Lose in

my ocations and affairs

June 15th, two pounds were allowed him on this petition.[8]
May 30th, 1705. Benjamin Church of Hadley, says:

> Haveing Rec^d a Wound in my Foot, in the fight at Derefeild Feb. 29, 1703 – 4. In the healeing of said wound, I was disabled for to work or labour for the space, or tyme, of twenty-five weeks, & am weak in my foot still * * * I entreat I may be been considered as aforesaid, & for your Excellency & Honors I shall Ever Pray.

Four pounds were allowed him, June 15th, I the Court."[9]
John Bridgman of Northampton was captured, but escaped to in the Meadow Fight. In a petition, May 22, 1705, he says:

> Being at Dearfeild upon the 29 day of faber, 1703–4, at the time when it was destroyed, & there meet with considerable Loss in estat, & maime it his body, being in her Majesty's service & under pay:
>
> ly I lost in goods, cloathing and money, to the value of five pounds eleven shillings & six pence.
>
> I was taken by the Enimy, & when I was in their hands, they cut off the forefinger of my Right hand,
>
> by which wound I Lost my time & was disenabled from work four months."

The items of loss were:

> Sadel 1 Pound 6s and od; leath^r breches, 15s; leathe^r wescot, 1 pound; gloves, 3s; leathe^r wescot, 16s; neckcloth & hankerchief, 6s; stockings, 4s; shirt, 5s; powder & lead, 2s, 6d; money, 14s.

Seven pounds were allowed him, June 26th, 1705.[10]

Stebbins-Related Aftermath

The Fitz John Winthrop Table of Losses[11] lists the Stebbins' losses as the death of Benoni Stebbins with the survival of 6 adults (including his wife) & 5 children, plus the capture of John Stebbins Jr with 6 other adults (including his wife) & 5 children.

At the time of his death Benoni was 51[12] The ages of John's family who ultimately found 'redemption' were: John Stebbins [Jr.] 56, Dorothy Stebbins 42(?), John Stebbins [III] 19, and Samuel Stebbins 15. John's family members who decided to stay in Canada after their capture, and thus were 'unredeemed' were: *Elizabeth Stebbins 20, Abigail Denio [De Noyon] 17, Thankful Stebbins 12, Ebenezer Stebbins 9, and Joseph Stebbins 4.[13]

* [There is sufficient doubt that Elizabeth was in reality Elizabeth Abigail Nims, who became a ward of the Stebbins family.]

Deerfield as a Military Post

We usually speak of the catastrophe of February 29th, 1704, as the 'destruction of Deerfield,' and rightly, too. For 20 years the persistent settlers had struggled bravely, not only against the inevitable hardships of a new plantation, but against the plague of worms, frost and drought; against war, pestilence, and almost famine. But the end had now come. The ground could be held no longer. They were but 25 men, 25 women, and 75 children, 43 of whom were under 10 years of age. More than half the population, including their loved minister, were being swept over the snow to Popish Canada, or laid underneath it, in one wide grave hard by in their own God's acre. Their cup was more than full; and this said despairing remnant, giving up all hope, deliberately resolved to abandon their all in this fatal spot; to let the 'candlestick of the Lord be removed,' and this speck of civilization become once more a waste place in the wilderness, from which they had tried to redeem it, while they sought refuge in the towns below. But fortunately, this broken people were not the arbiters of their own destiny. The policy of the rulers forbade the sacrifice.[14]

In 1694 an Act was passed, which continued during Queen Anne's War, prohibiting the desertion of frontier towns; even though many of their inhabitants had been killed or captured. A man could change his residence only by permission of the governor and council under pain of forfeiting his lands. Forasmuch as considerable sums had been expended in the defense and preservation of the out-towns and frontiers, it was enacted that they – naming eleven from Wells to Deerfield, and in later years increasing the number – should not be broken up, for if they were deserted without permission being given for "their drawing off," it would lessen the strength of the province and the enemy would be encouraged.[15]

Frontier towns, in his majesty's name, required all male persons capable of bearing arms to take their arms and ammunition 'to ye meeting-house evary Saboth day and at all other publick meetings,' and also into meadows and places where they worked, but if a man shot off a gun except at an Indian or a wolf he must forfeit 5 shillings, which amount he must also pay if he refused his above 'dewty.' Five shillings was the whole of the soldier's weekly wage, yet there may have been waste somewhere for Penhallow[16] says: 'The charge of war was so great that every Indian Massachusetts had killed or taken cost at least 1000 pounds.'[17]

Connecticut had usually responded promptly to calls for aid in defending Hampshire County. October, 1703, her General Court had established a Council of War, with authority to send 60 men in case of invasion. That number, and the 87 men more, arrived here before the close of March, 1704. A special session of the General Court of Connecticut convened March 15th, when 60 men were raised for permanent service in the county, in scouting and garrison duty. They soon came up under Capt. Benjamin Newberry. A committee came also to confer with Col. Partridge, how they could be employed to the best advantage. It was something more than neighborly kindness which prompted these efforts; it was in accordance with a wise policy of keeping the northern frontier as far as possible from their own borders. It was in pursuance of the same end, that Col. Partridge, on 2nd of March, forbade the inhabitants of our town to desert the place; and establishing here a military station, impressed all the able-bodied men as soldiers in the Queen's service. The non-combatants were sent to the lower towns.[18]

Gradually the men of Deerfield rallied from the great shock. By slow degrees, the situation took on a new aspect. Houses were left to shelter them; soldiers were there for their protection; the rich meadow land was still theirs. Their faith in an overruling Providence became once more a controlling power, and the future became more hopeful. Bravely they set about gathering up the broken threads of their lives as best they might.[19]

The house of the town clerk, Thomas French, though ransacked, was not burned, and the town books were preserved. On their time-stained pages bearing record of town action, there is not a single syllable referring to this great catastrophe. Those initiated, can see why the spring meeting was deferred 7 weeks; why the list of officers is incomplete; why a new handwriting appears on its pages. To other eyes nothing unusual is revealed. A meeting was held April 20th, when town clerk, selectmen, constable and fence viewers were chosen, and the machinery of a municipal organization so far set in motion. The functions of the constable were chiefly military: the fence was a necessity; for with stock running at large no crops could be raised on the Common Field unless this was in repair. Arrangements were made whereby 2 days out of 5 were allowed the impressed inhabitants by turns to labor in the fields. In this broken manner a small area of land was cultivated; but every hour thus spent was at the imminent risk of life. The woods were full of lurking Indians watching chances for spoil. Their first success is thus briefly recorded by Stephen Williams in his appendix to the 'Redeemed Captive.'[20]

May 11th, 1704, John Allen and his wife were killed at a place called the Bars." A manuscript account says Mrs. Allen was killed 'about a mile or two from the place.' Edward Allen, the new town clerk, a brother of John, makes this record: 'Joh Allyn, ye head of this famyly, was slaine by ye Enemy May ye 11, 1704.' He makes no note of the death of Mrs. Allen; by which it appears that her fate was then unknown. Her captors finding her an incumbrance in their hasty retreat, probably, knocked her on the head in the woods, where her body became the prey of wild beasts, the scalp being retained, to grace their triumphant reception at home. Allen was 44 years old.[21]

The next blow fell upon an outlying hamlet of Northampton, called Pascommuck, containing 5 families.[22]

Near the close of 1703, complaint was made to De Vandreuil, by the Penaski Indians, of losses by the English, and aid demanded. The governor at once sent Sieur de Montigny with 5 or 6 Frenchman to 'reassure them,' and 'engage them to continue the war' with the English. On the triumphant return of De Rouville from Deerfield, Montigny, with about 20 French, and 50 of these Indians, was sent to this valley to avenge their wrongs. May 13th, he surprised Pascommuck, and took all the inhabitants as prisoners. As soon as the captives could be secured, and provisions and plunder packed for the journey, De Montigny began his retreat.[23]

When the news of this disaster reached Northampton, Capt. John Taylor led a company of horsemen in pursuit, with a calamitous result, as we shall see. Whether or not the death strokes were actually given by the savages, the ordering of affairs was with Sieur De Montigny, the representative of France, 'who,' says Vaudreuil, 'distinguished himself particularly on that occasion.'[24]

The following account is taken from the Recorders Book for Old Hampshire County, which is relied upon as being an original record, though differing somewhat from the account given by Judd:[25]

> May 12, [13] Pascomok Fort taken by y[e] French & Indians, being about 72. They took and Captivated y[e] whole Garrison, being about 37 persons. The English pursuing of them cause them to nock all the Captives on the head save five or six. Three, they carried to Canada with them, the others escap'd and about 7 of those knocked on the head Recovered, y[e] rest died. Capt. John Taylor was killed in the fight, and Sam'l Bartlett wounded.[26]

Those carried to Canada were Esther, wife of Benoni Jones; her niece, Margaret Huggins, 18; and Elisha, son of John Searles, 8. The slain were Samuel James, 40, with wife Sarah, and children, Obadiah, Ebenezer, 3, Sarah, 1; 4 children of Benjamin Janes, Hannah, 8, Miriam, 4, Nathan, 1, and one of unknown name and age; Benoni Jones, about 35, with his children, Ebenezer, 6, and Jonathan, 1; John Searles, about 58, with 3 children, names and ages unknown; Moses Hutchison, and one child, and Patience Webb, 46, or her daughter Patience, 17.[27]

About a hundred miles up the valley, near the mouth of Wells river, was a tract of pine woods, called by the Indians Cowass, (place of pines) and nearby many acres of clear meadows. Here a party of Indians located a camp, and planted the meadows with corn, it being a convenient summer rendezvous, from which to sally out on the frontier. The captives from Pascommuck, and some of those from Deerfield were taken to the place. It was there in May, 1704, David Hoyt died of starvation. It was not far from there that Stephen Williams found Jacob Hickson, so weak from want of food, that he died before the end of July, at French river, while being taken to Canada. Rumors of the establishment of Cowass reaching the English, about the 6th June, a scouting party, made up of Caleb Lyman and five Connecticut Indians, was sent up to make an examination. On the 14th they discovered a camp about 20 miles this side of Cowass, which they surprised, and killed 6 men and 1 woman, while 2 others escaped, 1 mortally wounded. Making a hurried retreat, they reached home with six scalps in 5 or 6 days.[28]

The method of the English scout was exactly the same as that of the enemy. Coming near the Indian settlement, Lyman sent forth a spy, with his head and body covered with green leaves, to make what discovery he could. He found a wigwam not far away, and it was determined to attack it by night. Creeping on all fours, Lyman's party reached the wigwam undiscovered, and deliberately fired on the sleeping inmates. Then dropping their guns, 'we surrounded them,' says Lyman, 'with our clubs and hatchets, and knocked down several we met with.'[29]

No provisions were found, but loading the skins, guns and other plunder into the canoes, Lyman retreated down the river about 12 miles, when at daylight he broke up the canoes and took to the woods, knowing the parties of the in the enemy were between him and home. They had but 1 meal each in their packs, and lived on "birds, grass and strawberry leaves" until they reach Northampton, June 19th or 20th.[30]

The General Court gave Lyman 21 pounds and the Indians 10 pounds Major Whiting of Connecticut gave the Indians 40 pounds. This was repaid him by Massachusetts sometime after.[31]

When the Indians at Cowass heard the result of this foray, they deserted the place in alarm, and went off to Canada *via* French River and Lake Champlain. The Lyman scout proved to be a great and unexpected success. Great fears were entertained for their safety, for Lyman had hardly got away into the woods, before news came that an army was on the march from Canada to this valley. On this alarm Major Whiting came up from Connecticut with 342 men to aid in defending the frontier. Within 6 weeks, 2 more reports of the same nature followed, and each time, additional soldiers came up. These reports were true, the alarm well grounded, and the preparations timely and effective[32]

The Governor of Canada, elated by the success of De Rouville, had resolved 'to lay desolate all the places on the Connecticut river.' To this and he gathered a force of about 700 Indians, and adding 125 French soldiers, with several young and active officers, put the whole under Capt. De Beaucours, who set out for this valley soon after the return of Montigny from Pascommuck. There was great rejoicing in Canada on their departure. 'This force," says Vaudreuil, 'would be competent to attack whatever posts or village they please,' and he 'regarded as certain, the success of the expedition.' The Jesuits, says the captive John Williams, boasted what great things this army would do; 'that they could not devise what they should do with us, we should be so many prisoners when the army returned.' And yet, adds Mr. Williams, 'the great army turned back ashamed.' Probably they found our towns too much on the alert for a surprise, and they had no stomach for an open attack. De Vaudreuil, however, in his home report assigns another cause for this disgraceful retreat. He says, 'a French soldier, one Peter Newgate, deserted within a day's journey of the enemy; a panic hereupon seized the minds of our Indians to such a degree that it was impossible for Sieur de Beaucours to prevent them retreating.'[33]

While this Army lay on our frontiers it spies and scouts filled the woods, hovered about the towns, and waylaid the roads. Some of the results were given by Stephen Williams:

> About the middle of July [the 10th,] 1704, a friendly Indian was killed at Hatfield Mill. His name was Kindness. The enemy had not opportunity to scalp him. On the same week, Thomas Russell, a young man of Hatfield, (being then a soldier at Deerfield) was sent into ye woods with others as a scout, but he rambling from his company, was kill^d by ye Indians.
>
> Some tracks discover^d Deacon Sheldon wth some others went after y^m and came in sight of y^m, and shot at y^m, & y^y at ye english at a great distance, and then y^y past along on ye west side of ye Town, and fir^d y^r guns in a bravado, & went along up to ye Northward, & kill^d To^s Russell July 20, 1704.
>
> July 30, 1704, one Dr. Crossman with two or three More men were riding in the night between Hadley and Springfield & were fir^d upon by the enemy, who wound^d Dr. Crossman in the arm. This is ye only time (that I can learn) that they ever fir^d upon anybody traveling in the night.[34]

About this time, Sergt. John Hawks was fired upon while riding to Hatfield, and wounded in the hand. July 29th, Thomas Battis, who had been sent post to Boston, was killed on his return, east of Hadley. His dispatches were taken to Canada, and were the grounds on which Vaudreuil wrote the French war minister, in the report already quoted.

> Though this party broke up, it did not fail, My Lord, to cost the enemy considerable sums; the advices they received of it, having obliged them not only to postpone their meeting the Iroquois nations, but also, to remain a great portion of the summer idle, not knowing where this party might strike.[35]

July 31st, a scout was ambushed near Westfield, and two Connecticut soldiers, William Olmstead and one Benton, killed. Another English scout coming up soon after, killed in turn 2 of the Indians.[36]

No more depredations in the valley this year are recorded, but the harassing uncertainty spoken of by De Vaudreuil still kept the Connecticut troops here, and parties constantly scouting on the frontiers; it prevented labor in the fields, or any efficient action in getting a living. A strong garrison was kept here, and Benjamin Choate, a Harvard graduate of 1703, was sent here by the General Court to be 'chaplain to the Town and Garrison,' for 6 months from November 1st. He was continued here by the same authority until the return of Mr. Williams, on a salary of 40 pounds. Part of this was paid by the inhabitants.[37]

The country tax for 1703 – 4 was 68 pounds, 10s. Thomas Wells, Constable, received a warrant from the Treasurer, directing him to collect and send in that amount. One-half was paid in 1703; the rest was due in May, 1704. October 25th, 1704 the Constable sent a petition to the General Court, asking relief; saying 'the town was so far destroyed, that at least one-half that should be paid it, were killed were taken captive.' One-half of what was due in May was abated, and Col. Partridge, Preserved Smith, and Capt. Jonathan Wells, made a committee to reassess the balance of 17 pounds, 2s, 6d.[38]

As a preparation for a winter campaign, the General Court ordered, November 15th, that '5s be granted to every person who are or shall be furnished according to law with snow shoes and mogginsins.' Their necessity had been demonstrated at Deerfield, Feb. 29th, 1704; and two weeks later, 500 pairs had been ordered for frontier use. At that time the price was 3 shillings, which went up to 7 shillings before the war closed.[39]

Chapter 12

REDEMPTION OF CAPTIVES

Sheldon's First Expedition to Canada

In the efforts of the recovery and redemption of the captives from Canada, Ensign John Sheldon was a central figure. To his tenderness of heart, to his unflagging faith, his indomitable will, his muscles of iron and nerves of steel, is due in a large measure, the success which followed. His wife and her baby, his brother-in-law, and daughter's husband were slain. Four of his own children, his wife's brother with a large family, were in captivity. His house remained, but his hearthstone was desolate. The house of worship was spared, but the voice of his loved pastor was unheard within its walls. His colleague, Dea. Hoyt, was in captivity, and he alone was left to uphold the shattered church. Dea. Sheldon could get sympathy and Scriptural words of comfort to the bereaved, for he drank daily of the bitterness which flooded their souls; but unfitted for other sacerdotal duties, he mourned sadly for his pastor and friend, and pondered in his heart the possibilities of his redemption. Other public duties also devolved on this man. Ensign Sheldon was second in command of the garrison, and the incessant labors of that summer of fear and disaster, we have already seen. But as the season waned and the blasts of autumn laid bare the thickets which have been the coverts of the enemy, the danger lessened; and when Rev. Benjamin Choate was sent to be their chaplain and spiritual guide, in November, and the deacon was thus relieved of his ecclesiastical duties, he felt his presence less essential and a grand purpose gradually took form. He resolved to risk his life in a visit to his distressed children and friends in Canada. He could no longer endure the uncertainty hanging over their fate, which constantly haunted him. Had they met a lingering death, on the march, through hardship and privation? Or a sudden one by the merciful hatchet? Had their flesh been given to the wild beasts, and the bones left the bleach on some desolate Hill, or moulder in some dark morass? How many, and which, of their precious ones were dead? How many of the younglings of the flock were imbibing Popish poison in cruel bondage? These and similar questionings must be answered. Inspiring young John Wells (whose sister had been killed and mother captured) with like resolution, both set out for Boston, to get the necessary leave from the government.[1]

Dec. 13th, 1704, Gov. Dudley informed the Council that 'John Sheldon and John Wells of Deerfield, who both had relations in captivity, were now attending him, and very urgent to have liscense to travel thither.' On the 19th, he announced that Capt. John Livingstone of Albany, who was acquainted with the route by the lakes, was in town, and was willing to go with Sheldon and Wells for 100 pounds and his expenses. The Council advised his being employed, and the next day the 3 Johns, with credentials from the Governor, and letters to Marquis de Vaudreuil, took the Bay path for Hatfield, where they were fitted out for the journey by Col. Partridge. Their route was over the Hoosac Mountain to Albany, and thence northwards through the wilderness.[2]

In an historical sketch of Ensign John Sheldon, read before the Pocumtuck Valley Memorial Association, February 27th, 1878, C. Alice Baker says of this journey:

> We need not go back to King Arthur for exploits of chivalry; our colonial history is full of them. This man, long past that daring impulses of you, – this youth, whose life was all before him – show me to braver knights-errant setting out with loftier purpose, on a more perilous pilgrimage.
>
> Three hundred miles of painful and unaccustomed tramping on the snow-shoes in mid-winter, over mountain and morass, through tangled thickets and "snow-clogged forest," where with fell purpose the cruel savage lurked; with gun in hand and pack on back, now wading knee-deep over some rapid stream, now in the teeth of the fierce north wind, toiling over the slippery surface of the frozen lake, now shuffling tediously along in the sodden ice of some half-thawed river, digging away the drifts at night for his camp; wet, lame, half-famished, and chilled to the bone, hardly daring to build a fire, – a bit of dried

> meat from his pack for supper, spruce boughs for his bed, crouching there wrapped in his blanket, his head muffled in the hood of his capote, eye and ear alert, his mittened hand grasping the hilt of the knife at his belt; up at daybreak and on again, through the storm and sleep, pelted by pitiless rains, were blinded by whirling snow, – what iron will and nerves of steel, sound mind in sound body, to dare and do what this man did![3]

Slowly and warily, they traversed Lakes George and Champlain, down the Sorel to the St. Lawrence, and thence to Québec, where the worn travelers arrived without having been molested by savages. Here the minister and his deacon met. Here the latter heard the welcome news that his children and relatives were still alive, and the sad story of those who fell by the way, among whom was the mother of John Wells, his companion.[4]

The envoys were well received by De Vaudreuil, and encouraged to believe they would be successful in their mission. Mr. Williams, who had been sent down to 'Château-riche' [Château Richer] to prevent his hindering the Jesuits in their efforts to convert the captives to popery, had been allowed to come up to Québec. Every effort was made to learn about the prisoners and forward measures for their relief. The Jesuits who had great influence with Vaudreuil, obstructed the envoys in their mission in every possible way, and at their request, Mr. Williams was returned to Château Richer, after being at Québec but 3 weeks. 'One of chief note,' probably the intendant, invited Mr. Williams to dinner, where he was tempted with an offer to collect all the prisoners about him, and have a pension 'large enough for honorable maintenance for you and them,' if he would be of their religion. The Puritan replied, 'Sir, if I thought your religion to be true, I would embrace it freely, but so long as I believe it to be what it is, the offer of the whole world is of no more value to me than a blackberry.' His lordship then earnestly requested me, said Mr. Williams, 'to come down to the palace to-morrow morning and honor me with your company in my coach to the great church, it being then a saints day,' who replied, 'Ask me anything wherein I can serve you with good conscience, and I am ready to gratify you, but I must ask your excuse here.' It was after the Jesuits had given up all hope of any seeming compliance even, to their forms, that he was sent away from Québec.[5]

The apparently courteous reception of Mr. Sheldon really afforded him little opportunity of communication with the captives, but as his presence in Canada became known, 'it gave revival to many,' said Mr. Williams, 'and raised expectations of a return, * * * and strengthened many who were ready to faint, and give some check to the designs of the Papists to gain proselytes. But God's time of deliverance was not yet come.' The Indians feared an exchange of prisoners, when the French might take away their captives without ransom; so, they hustled them into hiding places, and pretended they were absent with hunting parties. March 29th, Mr. Sheldon received a letter from his son's wife enclosing the following note, probably from Mr. James Adams, who had been captured at Wells, by Beaubassin, August 10th, 1703:[6]

> I pray giue my kind loue to Landlord Shelden, and tel Him that I am sorry for all his los. I doe in these few lins showe youe that god has shone yo grat kindness and marcy, In carrying youre Daighter Hanna, and Mary in pertickeler, through so grat a iorney, far beiend my expectation, noing How Lame they war; the Rest of your children are with the Indians, Remembrance liues near cabect, Hannah also Liues with the frenc, Jn in the same house I doe.[7]

The reply of Vaudreuil to Dudley's proposal for an exchange of prisoners, was diplomatic and evasive, and nothing came of it.[8]

Meanwhile the envoys in Canada, by persistent endeavors, and the kindly aid of Capt. De Beauville, brother to the Lord Intendant, secured the release of Hannah Sheldon, and one of the other Ensign's children, Esther Williams and 2 others. Early in May, the whole party, escorted by Courtemanche and 8 French soldiers, set out for home by the way of Albany. Ostensibly this guard was sent as an act of honor and courtesy, but really to observe the condition of the enemy's territory. Livingstone and the escort were probably left at Albany, while Capt. Courtemanche and Ensign Sheldon pushed on to Boston, leaving the redeemed captives at Springfield, on the way. They arrived before June 5th, as appears by the General Court records. On that day, a committee was ordered to audit the accounts of the 'Messengers to Québec.' June 27th, they voted 'that an order be made on the Treasurer, payable forthwith to Vaudreuil's Commissioner for the amount,' taken up on their letter of credit, by Ensign Sheldon, which was 4000 livres. Courtemanche brought duplicates of the dispatches which Vaudreuil had sent Dudley by Samuel Hill, and another futile attempt was made to arrange an exchange of prisoners.[9]

Courtemanche being taken sick, Capt. Vetch with his brigantine, was engaged to take him home by sea. Capt. Hill was returned by the same conveyance. At the solicitation of the French envoy, William Dudley, son of the Governor, accompanying him to Québec. The latter bore new proposals to Vaudreuil for an exchange of captives. The vessel reached Québec in August and on the petition of Dudley and Vetch, Mr. Williams was allowed to go up and join them. He and his son Stephen were entertained by Courtemanche at his own house 'most nobly,' until September 19th, when he was sent back to Château Richer, because he hindered an English friar from making converts among the prisoners. Mr. Williams says the priests 'were ready to think their time was short for gaining English proselytes and doubled their diligence and wiles.'[10]

When Dudley arrived at Québec, Vaudreuil was at Montréal busy settling troubles among his Indian allies at the west, and on the 16th and 17th of August he was holding a conference with the Iroquois, who complained that while he had persuaded *them* to be neutral, their kindred in Canada [the Macquas] had been incited to take up the hatchet. The Governor defended his action as best he could, on the ground that it was necessary for them to make common cause with the Abenakis, who had been wronged by the English, and said that he must follow this course so long as the war between France and England continued. To the English envoys he held different language when he came down to Québec. He professed a great desire for peace, but found excuse for amending and returning the draft of the treaty brought by Dudley. He said the war could 'never contribute to the glory of their sovereigns, or the aggrandizement of their States, but merely to the ruin and desolation of some poor families,' and the priest at Château Richer told Mr. Williams he 'abhorred their sending down heathen to commit ravages against the English, saying that it was more like committing murders, then managing a war.'[11]

October 12th, Capt. Vetch sailed for Boston with young Dudley, where he arrived November 21st, having done little towards accomplishing the object of their mission, unless. as Ponchartrain, the French Minister, suspects, the illness of Courtemanche was a pretense, 'assumed as a cover for trade,' under an arrangement with Gov. Dudley. This conjecture appears more than probable, by the operations of Vetch the next year.[12]

The vessel, however, brought home 11 captives, only 3 of whom were known – Stephen Williams, Samuel Williams and Jonathan Hoyt. Nov. 30th, 1705, John Borland was allowed 22 pounds for their passage.[13]

Sheldon's Second Expedition to Canada

The Governor and Council could not accept the proposals brought from the Vaudreuil by Vetch, and the whole matter was left to Gov. Dudley, who was to advise with Lord Cornbury, Governor of New York. To forward the business of exchange, Dudley sent 47 French prisoners to Port Royal in December, and on the 17th of January 1705 – 6, he read to the Council his answer to Vaudreuil, which was 'to be dispatched to Québec by Mr. John Sheldon, attended with a servant or two, and accompanied by to French prisoners of war.' Mr. Sheldon left home January 15th and on the 17th he received an outfit from the Commissary General at Boston, costing 4 pounds, 11s, 6d, and a bill on Lewis Marchant of Québec for 2 pounds, 10s; and for John Wells, on the same service. 16s, 6d. Joseph Bradley of Haverhill, it seems, got leave to attend the envoy as one of the servants. His wife was now in second captivity in Canada. January 20th, Sheldon bearing funds to the military chest in the valley, with Bradley, and two Frenchman, left Boston for Hadley, where they arrived the next day, as shown by the following paper:[14]

> Rec'd of Deacon Shelding this Jan'ie 21, 1705, three hundred forty-one pounds eight shillings & one penny w[ch] s[d] sum he Rec'd of Mr. James Taylor, Treasu'r in Boston, & Brought & delivered to me as aboovs[d], w[ch] I own I have the day of the date aboovs[d] Received.
>
> per me,
> Sam'll Partridge[15]

John Wells joined the party at Deerfield, and on the 25th of January, 1706, the ambassador plunged once more into the wilderness for a winter journey to Canada. His experience now aided him in battling with the elements, and a truce which had been arranged for 5 weeks, secured him from the Indian hostility, and thus enabled him to push on more rapidly and so arrive before its expiration.[16]

April 28th, 1706, De Vaudreuil writes to Ponchartrain, enclosing Dudley's propositions by Capt. Vetch, and his own reply; with account of the attempt to arrange a treaty of neutrality. He says:[17]

> This induced Mr. Dudley to send me, a Deputy by land, with a letter, about a month ago, but as it is not sufficiently explicit as Mr. Dudley according to occurrences is seeking only to gain time, the term I had fixed in my answer to these propositions having expired, I permitted several small parties of our Indians to recommence hostilities.[18]

This deputy was Ensign Sheldon, but Mr. Williams says the ensign reached Québec 'the beginning of March.' On his arrival he was glad to find Mr. Williams; but in a few days the latter was sent down to Château Richer, and Sheldon was left alone two prosecute his mission, which he found difficult and perplexing. Dudley's dispatches were not satisfactory to Vaudreuil. The Jesuits use their all-powerful influence for delay, and redoubled their artful efforts to seduce the young captives to popery. The sturdy envoy persisted in pushing his claims to at least as many captives as would equal the French prisoners which Dudley had sent to Port Royal, in December, 1705; and he so far succeeded, that on 30th May, he embarked for Boston with 44 English captives, onboard the French vessel La Marie, chartered at an expensive 3000 livrers, for Port Royal and Boston. After considerable delay at Port Royal, he reached his destination August 2d, 1706.[19]

In this company came James Adams of Wells, Hannah, wife of Joseph Bradley, – one of Sheldon's attendants, Ebenezer (?) and Remembrance, sons of Ensign Sheldon, and his daughter Mary, Thomas French, Sen., John Burt, Benjamin Burt, his wife Sarah, and their children, Christopher, born April 4, 1704, while on the march to Canada, and Seaborne, born July 4, 1706, on the home voyage. Mrs. Mary Hinsdale gave birth to son Ebenezer, on the voyage. Both babies were baptized by Samuel Willard, on landing in Boston. The names of the others are unknown, but the greater number were presumably Deerfield captives. August 8th, with light hearts, these began their homeward march.[20]

Mr. Williams not being allowed to see the assembled company of returning captives, wrote them a 'Pastoral Letter,' dated at Château Richer, May 28th, 1706. It was sent on board, 'Per Samuel Scammon, Q.D.C. Present with care I pray.' This was to be read to his flock on the homeward voyage. He says:[21]

> Inasmuch as I may neither be permitted to return with you; nor be permitted to come to see you before your return; these come to acquaint you that I am truly desir-

> ous of Prosperity for soul and Body. I would bless God who was opening a door of Return for you; and if God be your Front Guard & Rearward, it shall go well with you. * * * Pray for us that are left behind, that God would preserved and recover us, and give us Grace to Glorify His Holy name, tho' He continue, yea increase our Trials*** What is it that is most upon your heart in your Return? Is it that you may with all Freedom Glorify God, and bringing forth much Fruit, whilst you are again planted in the Court Yards of our God? How sorrowful is it if your greatest design be to see your Friends so long Separated from you; to Gain Estates, and recover your outward Losses; and to be free again to go and come as you list![22]

This is the spirit of the whole address. He urges them to make it a business to glorify God.[23]

> Let God have the Glory of preserving you, and don't ascribe it to your own wisdom; don't think to go shares or partners with God in His Glory; he has done it for the honor of His Name * * * Don't think after your return; that having desired publicly in the congregation of God's people to have thanks returned to God on your behalf; you have done your duty * * * *Thanksliving is the best Thanksgiving.* * * * I wish you a healthy, safe, a speedy passage to your destined port; if it be the will of God. But above all, I wish you a gracious truly penitent, Christ prizing, and soul enriching, sanctifying voyage to a better port, when it is the pleasure of God to call you to come home to your Father's house.[24]

Zedediah Williams, captured in the Deerfield Meadows, Oct. 8th, 1703, died in the hospital at Québec, April 12th, 1706. Mr. Williams says: 'He was a very hopeful and pious young man, prayerful to God and studious and painful in reading the Holy Scriptures.'[25]

Williams had 'recovered one, [Joseph Edgerly] fallen to Popery,' and after his death, the French told Mr. Williams, 'Zebediah was gone to hell and damned, for he had appeared to Joseph Edgerly in a flame of fire, and told him he was damned for refusing to embrace the Romish religion, when such pains were used to bring him to the true faith, and being instrumental in drawing him from the Romish communion – forsaking the mass – and was therefore now come to advertise him of his danger.' 'I told them,' says the plainspoken Mr. Williams, 'I judged it to be a Popish lie!' and he soberly went about gathering evidence to prove it so; and wrote to Samuel Webb Hill and his brother Ebenezer, at Québec, 'to make discovery of this lying plot, to warn them of their danger.' It seems he seriously feared its effect upon the superstitious minds of his flock.[26]

The successful mission of Ensign Sheldon having opened the door for the captives' return, the brigantine Hope, Capt. Bonner, was chartered to bring another party of them home. August 9th, an order was issued by the General Court that the captain of the La Marie be kept under inspection, and that the French prisoners be gathered at once at Cambridge, ready to be sent home when the vessel was ready. These prisoners had probably been scattered among the towns.[27]

Envoy John Sheldon, ensign and deacon, was constable as well, as soon as his papers were presented and reports made to the Governor, he hastened home and Aug. 27th, he was fitting out these men to join the other French captives now being gathered at Cambridge for the home voyage.[28]

The brigantine Hope and La Marie, with Capt. Samuel Appleton as agent, sailed for Québec with the French prisoners soon after, reaching their port about October 1st. Then came a trying struggle between the French priests and Mr. Williams for the possession of the captive children. 'I cannot tell you,' says he, 'how the clergy and others labored to stop many of the prisoners. To some liberty, to some money and yearly pensions were offered, if they would stay.' To some they urged the danger of shipwreck at that late season, and "some younger ones they told 'if they went home, they would be damned and burnt in hell forever,' to afright them.' To Mr. Williams's son Warham, then 7 years old, they promised 'an honorable pension from the King,' and a 'great deal' from his master, 'an old man, and the richest in Canada.' No means was left untried to prevail upon them to stay 'at least till spring. * * * But God graciously brake the snare, and brought them out.'[29]

Who can imagine the anxiety and distress of the good pastor in this critical time? or the intense feeling of relief, when the strain was removed, and Hope spread her white wings over 57 English captives for the homeward voyage, and his lambs were safe and beyond the reach of the Popish wolves? They sailed October 25th and had a narrow escape from shipwreck shortly after; but arrived safely at Boston on the 21st

November, 1706. On landing they were sent for to go before the General Court, which voted that "20 shillings be allowed each prisoner this day returned from captivity." Capt. Appleton's bill of expenses being 1406 pounds, six shillings, was allowed December 6th; amongst the items of his bill were 2 pounds, 13 s, 6d, for 5 Bibles sent to the captives, and 155 livers paid for the redemption of 3 captives. This sum was probably to reimburse the French for what they paid the Indians as the price of the captives; Dudley having firmly resolved not to 'set up an Algiers trade,' purchasing the captives from the Indians, as such a course would and surely encourage them to further raids.[30]

December 6th, the General Court voted Mr. Williams 40 pounds on condition that he returned to Deerfield within 3 weeks and remained a year.[31]

Of all the 57 captives who returned with Appleton, the names of only Mr. Williams and his children Esther and Warham are known.[32]

Sheldon's Third Expedition to Canada

Their being still many English captives in Canada whom Vaudreuil has promised return in the spring. Dudley proposed to the Council, January 14th, 1707, to have 'a Person Ledger at Québec, to put forward that affair, and Mr. John Sheldon, who has been twice already, may be employed with a suitable retinue to undertake a journey thither on that service.' This plan was adopted: Two men of character and standing, Edward Allen, town clerk of Deerfield and Deacon Edmund Rice of Sudbury, were elected as a 'suitable retinue.' Nathaniel Brooks, a Deerfield captive, was added somewhere on the route. It was now a time of active hostilities, and this embassy though ever so wise and prudent, ran great risks. They might at any time be fired upon from some cover before their flag of truce was seen or their character discovered."[33]

They set out April 17th, and arrived at Québec May 9th without molestation. In a dispatch to Dudley of June 20th, Sheldon says they found the city in a fever of excitement, over news of an expedition fitting out in New England against Canada, and active in preparations to repel it. Their presence was un-welcome and the 'Ledger' found a less courteous reception than his former visits. He was not imprisoned, but was kept under strict surveillance and not allowed to go home lest he report the condition of their defenses and military preparations. After about 6 weeks at Québec, he was sent up to Montréal. Col. Schuyler writing to Col. Partridge, Aug. 11th, 1707, tells him that his Indian spies, just returned, report that 'they see Deacon Sheldon at Montréal, who walked the streets, but was told he was detained, and had not the liberty to go home.' We find no details of the negotiations for prisoners, for which there could have been but scant opportunity, in this crisis. Within 3 weeks after Sheldon's arrival an English Army had made an attack on Port Royal. The event of the campaign being determined, the embassy was allowed to depart.[34]

On the 11th August, Sheldon, bearing dispatches of August 16th, [N. S.,] from Vaudreuil to Dudley, set out from Chambly. He was escorted by 5 French soldiers under Capt. de Chambly, a brother of Hertel de Rouville. They arrived at Albany August 24th, whence Sheldon wrote the Council a letter, received September 2d, in which he says 'Col. Schuyler had obliged him, with the 6 Frenchman, to attend the Lord Cornbury, at New York.' This was no hardship for the Frenchman; and he gave them greater facilities for carrying out their secret instructions. Vaudreuil gave a detailed account of this mission in his dispatches to the home government. In reply, Ponchartrain, the war minister, says:[35]

> His Majesty approves of your haven spoken as you have done to the man name Schalden [Sheldon] whom that Governor [Dudley] sent to you overland inquest of the English press prisoners at Québec, and even had you imprisoned him, and those of his suite, it would have been no great harm. You did well to send those prisoners to Orange, under the charge of an officer, and a detachment of soldiers, and to recommend that officer to inform himself of what was passing at Orange, and in countries in that direction, in possession of the English.[36]

Leaving New York, Sheldon's party traveled eastward, by Saybrook, New London and Seeconk, reaching Boston September 8th, when Sheldon delivered his dispatches to the Governor, and gave the Council a verbal account of his mission. He soon after went home. In October, he was sent again to Boston as an agent for the town.[37]

The names of the captives brought home by Mr. Sheldon on this ill-timed mission are unknown, save as gathered from the foregoing petition and bill. Nathaniel Brooks was from Deerfield. His two children were left behind; their mother had been killed on the March. Henry Seger was son of Henry of Newtown. Of the Woodbury woman and the mulatto nothing further appears.[38]

Such facts as have been found relating to the captives from Deerfield who remained in Canada, will be given as a contribution to their history. The list made up by Stephen Williams about 1730, and printed in Prince's edition of the 'Redeemed Captive,' may be referred to in this connection.[39]

Although Williams extolled 'the kindness of the Lord' in making safe the captives' return, God had frowned as well. By Williams's own estimate, a 'great number' of New Englanders remained in Canada, 'not much short of a 100.' Included in this total was a large group from Deerfield. Of the 109 prisoners taken from the town 3 years before, 88 had survived the journey to Canada. Of these 59 had come home – yet 29 remained behind.[40]

The 29 were especially painful group to lose, for they were the young. Consistent with the pattern seen throughout the colonial wars, the French and Indians particularly wanted to keep children. They were the easiest to control, to convert, and to integrate into society, whether Indian or French. John Williams claimed that the French work particularly hard to 'seduce our young ones. Some, he explained 'were sent away [set free] who were judged ungainable, [but] most of the younger sort still kept, some still flattered with promises of reward.' The results were painfully effective. All of Deerfield's 29 unredeemed captives were under 20 years of age; what's more, 15 of the 18 girls were under 12 and 9 of the 11 boys under 14, generally the pivotal ages in ages in deciding whether to keep youths.[41]

Chapter 13

THE CLOSE OF QUEEN ANNE'S WAR

1705

This year no enemy appeared on our borders. Vaudreuil was crippled by the loss of the 'Seine,' his annual store ship of supplies, with 'two-millions of wealth.' It was captured by the British in October, 1704. The Bishop of Canada, with 20 ecclesiastics were on board. It was a severe blow to the enemy. Negotiations for treaty of neutrality was set on foot this year, pending which, there was less disposition for hostile action. There were several alarms here, however, and much marching of troops, and continuous scouting.[1]

1706

During the negotiations between Gov. Dudley and De Vaudreuil for exchange of prisoners and treaty of neutrality, there was a general desire for peace on the part of the English. Dudley evidently did not share this feeling. He was ambitious for the conquest of Canada; and his policy seems to have been, to prolong the correspondence until he could recover the captives in the hands of the enemy, and gain time and opportunity to affect his object. During this same period, Vaudreuil, who had become alarmed for the safety of Canada, and therefore desirous of peace, sent no parties of Indians against our valley. The vigilance of our authorities, however, was not relaxed. A garrison constantly occupied Deerfield, and scouts were kept ranging in the woods.[2]

When the joyful news reached Deerfield of the return of Mr. Williams to Boston a town meeting was at once called. By the record of its action the town's relation to the Redeemed Captive seems a little mixed. He is called their pastor, and at the same time measures were adopted for his *resettlement*. There may have been no precedents to govern the case.[3]

A conference with 'the Elders' probably showed the fact, that no special 'management' was necessary, and Mr. Williams was soon reestablished in his chosen work, and field of labor, without further ceremony, having refused eligible offers of settlements near Boston.[4]

From the day of her great disaster, up to this time, Deerfield had hardly been more than a military post, held by soldiers in pay of the colony; and little attention had been given to municipal affairs beyond keeping up the meadow fence. The discouraged inhabitants had felt that at any time they might be called upon to desert the place. Now, everything was changed. Their loved minister, who had been so much to them, was again among them. Their courage rose. The town should now be held at all hazard; and the regular routine of town business must be taken up. First of all, Mr. Williams must be provided for.[5] [Jan. 9, 1706-7 they voted to build him a house.]

1707

That all land owners should bear their share of the burdens, a petition was sent to the General Court for leave 'to rais all thair town charges upon lands only.'[6]

The military defenses had become so weak that the labor necessary to strengthen the lines was more than the settlers could bear, and a call was made upon Col. Partridge for aid.[7]

June 13th, 1707, 30 pounds was 'allowed towards the part of the general fortification, that falls to the share of the poor of Deerfield, and such as are returned from captivity.'[8]

This appropriation, it will be observed, was for the general stockade. No more is heard of the smaller work of square timber proposed by Col. Partridge.[9]

August 11th, 1707, Col. Schuyler wrote Partridge, that his Indian spies, just returned from Canada, reported a party of 27 French and Indians at the mouth of Otter Creek on the 6th, bound for the New England frontier. The spies were charged by this party not to tell of the expedition. To this they would not agree, as the war party 'was going to kill our brethren of New England.' Nothing more was heard of these enemies. Probably this discovery sent them back. No Indian made an attack but by surprise; according to their ethics, it would be a disgrace to do it openly.[10]

In this war the English adopted the French tactics, and sent small scouts to harass the frontiers of the enemy. From the following paper a good idea of their methods may be obtained:[11]

> Capt. [John] Stoddard set away from Deerfield on 28th April with 12 men, & Wednesday was a fortnight after, they tracked Indians upon the French River & they followed them till Saturday night at which time they had got to the last carrying place, and was quite discouraged & concluded that they had got so far out of their Reach y^t y^a could not overtake y^m & three of them had a mind to take their cano, which was all they had that was serviceable and go to Chamblee and get a Frenchman, or more if they could, and set away upon the lakes & was driven by a contrary wind upon a point of land; & there they discovered some Indians; & two of y^m staid at ye canno, and third, namely, John Wells, went to observe their motions & after he had got a little way he saw a person with its back toward him, he being in a plain place so that he could not get away without being discovered, & he was loath to shoot, because he was in hopes of getting more booty, & while he was thus thinking the person rose up & stood a little while & for fear of being discovered he shot & she fell down; he took his hatchet out of his girdle & ran up to it to cut off its head & then he saw it had a white face, which very much startled him, & she spake saying, "Netop, Netop, my master." He ran to the cano; they set off; the Indians shot off two or three guns which he judged were to alarm one another, and they overtook ye rest of y^{ir} company ye same day just at night & they y^{it} set away for home & arrived the 30th of May. By the discribing of the person y^t was killed Uncle thinks it was an Eastern captive, namely Johannah Ardaway, and Wells saith y^t he thought it was she, as soon as he saw her face.[12]

1708

At a meeting Feb. 1st, 3 men 'were chosen a Committee to Masure all ye common fence in Derefield and to stake it out to ye now present proprietors.'[13]

Although 1708 was a year of alarm and disaster, the above are the only allusion on the town record to anything connected with the war; what I have learned of military operations about this period, has been found chiefly in English and French official reports.[14]

About the first of February, 1708, news was received through Col. Schuyler, that a large force had been fitted out in Canada to begin a march against this region January 15th. Active measures were once taken for defense. Connecticut was appealed to, and sent up Col. William Whiting with several companies of infantry and dragoons. The first week in February Capt. Benjamin Wright led a party of English and Indians up the Connecticut. He went as high as Cowass; was gone about 9 weeks and returned without seeing the face of the enemy. Scouts were kept constantly out in other directions. The warning and preparation probably prevented that attack. Small parties hovered about the frontiers, however, all the season, keeping up the alarm, preventing any labor in the field except under strong guards.[15]

July 9th, one of these parties killed and scalped Samuel and Joseph Parsons, sons of Capt. John Parsons, at Northampton. July 26th, the house of Lieut. Abel Wright of Skipmuck (now Chicopee) was surprised. Aaron Parsons and Barijah Hubbard were killed and their bodies mangled; Martha, wife of Lieut. Wright, was mortally wounded. Two grandchildren, Hannah, age 2 years and, and Henry, 7 months, lying in a cradle together, were Tomahawked. Hannah survived the blow. Her mother, wife of Henry Wright, was captured and never afterwards heard from.[16]

August 5th, Col. Peter Schuyler writes Gov. Dudley that an army was being assembled at Montréal, and that he was trying to find out their design. The next day he sends news that 800 men were on a march for New England. The express bearing this information arrived at Boston on the 10th. The soldiers were put under marching orders, and the woods filled with scouts, to learn the point of attack.[17]

De Vaudreuil had been blamed by the home government for beginning this war with the English colonies. He was now urged to prosecute it more vigorously. Pontchartrain the war minister, wrote him June 30th, 1707, to send out more parties to harass the English, adding, 'if you could go out and attack them yourself, his Majesty would be glad of it;' and, again, that the king 'expected to receive news of some expedition against them, and is not satisfied with the inactivity in which you remain, with such numerous forces as you have.' In accordance with his directions De Vaudreuil had raised a large army of French and Indians, and put Hertel de Rouville at its head.[18]

De Rouville began his march July 16th. To conceal his destination, part of the force went up the St. Francis river and the rest up the Sorel, to Lake Champlain. The latter were mostly French Mohawks or Macquas, over whom Col. Schuyler had great influence. On the march they met Schuyler's messengers, bearing a secret belt, desiring them not to go to war against the English. The Macquas, pretending to the French that some infectious disease had appeared among them, at once turned back and went home.[19]

A large portion of the Indians with the other part of the army also deserted. The plan of the campaign was, for both branches to unite in an attack on the Maine coast, with force enough to sweep all before it. On the desertion of the Macquas, De Vaudreuil ordered De Rouville to push on with his Frenchman and St. Francis Indians, and surprise some scattered settlement. Henceforth, the barbarous murder of frontier settlers was to please the King of France, as well as the Abenakis.[20]

August 23rd, Dudley received word from Schuyler, that the Indians had turned back, and that there was nothing to fear from the French, who could do nothing without them. On this representation part of the soldiers were dismissed, including a force of 500 volunteers under officers of their own choice.[21]

Meanwhile De Rouville had traversed 3 or 4 hundred miles of forest, and at daybreak on 29th of August, he surprised the town of Haverhill, killed about 40 of the inhabitants and took many captives. He began his retreat about sunrise, but was pursued by the survivors, who attacked him, killed his brother, another French officer, and 7 men; took a third officer prisoner, and rescue part of the captives. In the north part of the township, Joseph Bradley – the same who accompanied Ensign Sheldon to Canada – hearing the alarm, collected a party and sallied out into the woods. He discovered and secured the medicine chest of the invaders, and their knapsacks, which they had taken off before making the assault. It was feared De Rouville would now turn to the Connecticut Valley, and Aug. 31st, the Council sent orders to Col. Partridge to prepare for their reception. A large force came up from Connecticut, and the military companies made ready to march at a moment's warning. Nothing more was seen of De Rouville, but some of his Indians may have remained upon our frontiers.[22]

About this time a scout of 6 men from Deerfield fell into an ambush of Indians near Cowass. Martin Kellogg, after shooting one of the enemy, was taken captive the second time. A son of Josiah Barber of Windsor Conn., after receiving a fatal wound, rallied and getting on his knees, shot the Indian who had fired upon him. Both were found dead by the Indians, shortly after, lying but a few rods apart. The Indian who told this story of Barber's pluck to Stephen Williams, added, 'no *he,* (i.e. Barber) but *his ghost*,' did the exploit.[23]

Oct. 13th, Abijah Bartlett was killed at Brookfield and Joseph and Benjamin Jennings, and John Green, wounded, and John Walcott, a lad of 10, captured.[24]

October 26th Ebenezer Field of Hatfield was killed at Bloody Brook, while on his way to this place. With his death, the tragedies of the year closed. There could, however, be no relief from the anxiety, watching, warding and scouting. The enemy might strike again at any moment. On receiving the report of this year's operations, the King wrote De Vandreuil that he was satisfied with his application.[25]

1709

During the winter of 1708-9, there was a great alarm in Canada upon a report received by Sieur de Joncaire, through the Mohawks, that an English Army was coming over the snow against Montréal. De Vaudreuil, with all regular soldiers, took post at the threatened point, and all the militia were under orders to march at a moment's warning. De Vaudreuil remained in this posture of defense about a month; meanwhile, fortifications were being made in every direction. Quiet was hardly restored before the scare was repeated. This time the grounds of alarm were real. Gen. Nicholson with 1500 man was moving from Albany toward Lake Champlain. April 27th, De Vaudreuil returned to Montréal, where an army was collected, to repel the invaders. Orders were issued to gather all the inhabitants and movable property from the south of the St. Lawrence within the walls of Montréal and Québec, and on the north side to drive the cattle and remove the women and children up into the forests northward. The walls of Québec were strengthened in every possible way, the settlers were called from their farms, and much of the harvest was lost for the lack of hands to gather it. De Vaudreuil had 'sure news' of an intended attack both by sea and land, and the whole spring and summer was spent in preparations to resist it. On the other hand, the English army halted at Wood Creek, waiting until October for the arrival of the fleet which was expected to assail Québec, while Nicholson went against Montréal. Three forts were built meantime and hundreds of bateaux and canoes in which to cross the lake.[26]

Scouts from each frontier were sent against the other, seeking prisoners and information of military movements. In this the French had the earliest success.[27]

On the return of De Rouville and De la Periere to Canada *via* the lakes, with reports of the condition of affairs at Wood Creek, De Vaudreuil sent Sieur de Ramezay, Governor of Montréal, with 1500 French and Indians, up Champlain to surprise the English. They left Chambly about 17th of July, and being discovered when they had arrived near Crown Point by an advanced guard of Nicholson's army, they retreated after slight skirmish.[28]

The alarm in Canada now became almost a panic. All possible measures for defense were taken. No more war parties were sent against our frontiers; but 1 already out killed John Clary and Robert Granger, at Brookfield, on the 8th of August.[29]

Gen. Nicholson, tiring of waiting for the fleet, left Wood Creek, September 26th, to consult with the colonial governments as to what measures to take. Shortly after, the whole army retired to Albany, burning their forts and boats as they retreated. The expected ships had gone to Portugal, and all the trouble and expense in preparing for the campaign was thrown away. Rev. John Williams was chaplain in this futile expedition, and received 24 pounds, 8 shillings, sixpence for his time and expenses. During his absence, 'Mr. John Avery and Mr. Aaron Porter' were chaplains by turn at Deerfield, and were paid 10 pounds each for the service.[30]

Thomas [French] and his children; Mary, 17; Thomas, 14; Freedom, 11; Martha, 8; and Abigail, 6; made the long journey. He and his 2 eldest children were redeemed in 1706. Three years later he married Hannah [Atkinson], the widow of Benoni Stebbins. He died in 1733.[31]

1710

In the winter of 1709-10, De Vaudreuil, under a pretext of exchanging prisoners, but really as he writes to France, 'to obtain information of what is going on at Orange,' sent Sieurs de la Periere and Dupuis, with 5 men to Albany, as escort for Lieut. Staats, a nephew of Col. Shuyler, and 3 other Dutch prisoners, to be exchanged for Father de

Manreuil, and 3 other Frenchman; they also brought 'a militia officer of the Boston government,' to exchange for 'Sieur de Vercheres, ensign of the Regulars.' This 'militia officer' was John Arms of Deerfield, captured the June previous. One of the French officers probably came with Arms to Deerfield. The dispatches brought from Canada were forwarded to Boston by Col. Partridge. Gov. Dudley is displeased with these proceedings, and writes to Partridge in February that he believes these officers little better than spies, and directing him to send them back, and Arms with them. He said he is ready to exchange prisoners when the French follow the course agreed upon. The French officers reach Montréal on their return about the 'time navigation opened.' Arms appears to have been left on parole.[32]

A few weeks previous, Dudley had written in reference to the ransom of Josiah Littlefield, of Maine: 'I always pitty a prisoner in Indian hands, especially when their masters are indigent, in necessity of everything; but no consideration of that nature has yet altered my resolution never to buy a prisoner of and Indian, lest we make a market for our poor women and children in the frontiers.' He had also in this case, prevented the goods which Littlefield had himself ordered for his own ransom, from being forwarded to his Indian master.[33]

On learning the decision of the Governor and Council, John Arms at once hurried to Boston, armed with letters for Mr. Williams, his minister, and Col. Partridge, seeking to avert the hard fate of being returned to Canadian captivity. He appeared before the Council March 6th, to plead his cause in person; but his mission was fruitless; the policy of the government was fixed, and he 'was dismissed, the Governor and Counsel not seeing reason to alter anything of their directions to Col. Partridge by their letters last week.' Notwithstanding this decision, our townsman did not return with the French officers.[34]

The measures Arms took to secure his freedom have not been discovered. It would seem that he had been captive to the Indians, and that a 'French captain' had ransomed him for 100 livres, which he had obligated himself to repay. Arms was also held as a prisoner of war, and a French officer of the line was asked in exchange. This officer, whose name is given as Sieur de Vercheres,' by De Vaudreuil and 'Le Fever' by Dudley, did not return with the French envoys. A prisoner of the latter name was at Hadley two years later, when he refused to return with a party exchanged prisoners going from Deerfield to Canada, and declared his intention of becoming a citizen.[35]

Arms was allowed 6 pounds, 6 shillings, on his bill of May 27th. He became a cripple from his wounds, and a life pension of 6 pounds a year was granted him in

1721, to which 3 pounds, 10 shillings was added in 1752.[36]

August 10th, 1710, Connecticut voted to raise scouting parties, not to exceed 60 Indians and 4 or 5 English, to range toward the lakes; fitting them out and paying a bounty of 10 pounds for each Indians scalp. Of all the troubles from the enemy this year, not a clue is found on the town records, although the action of 3 meetings is recorded.[37]

1711

This year another attempt was made to subdue Canada. Fifteen men of war and 40 transports sailed from Boston, July 30th, for Québec. Ten transports and a thousand men were lost by shipwreck in the St. Lawrence August 21st, and the rest turned back. Another army of 4000 men was collected on the old ground above Albany under Gen. Nicholson, but nothing was accomplished against Canada. Rev. John Williams was chaplain on this expedition. The campaign was a total failure except so far as it kept the enemy away from our frontiers. The only loss in the valley was at Northampton, August 10th or 11th, when Samuel Strong was killed and his father Samuel wounded and taken captive.[38]

December was a cold month; the snow was deep, the rivers and lakes were frozen very hard, and an expedition from Canada was feared. December 27th, Connecticut voted that 'a small scout of 10 or 12 men be posted about 30 or 40 miles above Deerfield upon some eminence for the discovery of the enemy until such time as the approach of the spring renders it impractical for them to come in a body.'[39]

1712

As an additional security, Col. Partridge sent a large force up here January 9th, provided with snowshoes, and prepared for a winter's campaign. Two companies of snowshoe men were sent from the Bay, to be employed by Col. Partridge for the defense of Hampshire County, 'particularly by posting some of them in conjunction with such as Col. Partridge shall joyn with them, in some convenient place or places, above the scout now stated 30 miles above Deerfield, to discover the approach of the enemy.'[40]

March 12th, Lieut. William Crocker was directed to raise a party of English and Indian volunteers to join the scout that Partridge was fitting out, to send 'up to Coaset to meet the Indian enemy hunting in these parts.' No further account of this most remarkable winter's campaign has been found. No details of the endurance, bravery and heroism of those men who spent the dead of winter in tramping through the forests and camping on the mountains of Southern Vermont; waiting and watching the approach of the subtle foe, while their lives depended on their ability to outmatch in strategy an enemy with a life-long training in the arts of wood-craft. The number of men engaged is not known, but in the spring, Col. Partridge was allowed 7 shillings for each of the 468 pairs of snowshoes and moccasins furnished to that number of men.[41]

There had been no general exchange of prisoners since John Sheldon was in Canada. Individual or special exchanges have been made occasionally, perhaps as one side or the other took that method of gaining intelligence of the enemy.[42]

June 16th, a letter was received from De Vaudreuil respecting an exchange of prisoners of war. He proposes 'that our prisoners from Canada be brought into or near Deerfield, and that the French prisoners be sent home from thence.' This proposal is satisfactory to Dudley, and Col. Partridge was ordered to collect the prisoners here and dispatch them home. Partridge set about the mission with zeal and energy and in about 4 weeks, a party of French captives, with an English escort, left Deerfield under a flag of truce for Canada. The departure had been delayed somewhat by difficulty from an unexpected quarter.[43]

The party left for Canada left Deerfield July 10th, with Lieut. Samuel Williams finally at the head.[44]

Lieut. Williams reached Boston on his return September 24th, bringing 9 English prisoners. He was allowed 30 shillings per week. Lieut. Williams, son of the minister, was but 23 years old. In March, 1713, he was chosen town clerk, and died in June following.[45]

The quiet ... was soon to be broken. On July 13th, 20 Indians in 2 parties left Canada for our frontiers; 12 under the noted Greylock. The news of this movement reached Col. Schuyler July 28th. He sent a post in hot haste to warn Col. Partridge; but it was too late. Partridge writes the Governor August 4th:[46]

Hatfield August 4, 1712

The Dead 1704

May please yoʳ Excellency

On Wednesday the 30 July past in yᵉ forenoone came to me a Messengʳ enforming of a young man taken by a pᵗⁱᵉ of the Enemy at Springfield in the afternoone a messenger from Derefᵈ that oʳ western scout from thence was attacqued by the enemy & sᵈ ther were most of them taken & killed, but upon a more full accᵗ there is one man killed & two taken of them, at Night a Messenger from oʳ Eastern scouts gave news of the discovery of a pᵗⁱᵉ of 8 or 9 seen & they made shot at yᵐ but the the enemy soon ran out of reach towards Brookfᵈ We immeadiately sent a post to Brookfᵈ to enforme them, who immeadiately sent out there all there work folks abroad & in there way see 6 or 8 Indians – Alarmed the yᵉ said workers & disappointed the Enemy who were about Secretly to way lay them, but run for it – by all this it plainly appears the Enemy are on every hand of us – Laying waite for to accomplish their bloody designes – the same night a post from Albany came from the Enclosed, The lettʳ doth not speak of it, but the Missingʳˢ say yᵉ Govʳ of Canada Looks for a speedy Peace, but will do as much spoyle as he can before it comes.

I have Given Notice to Capt. How of the Enemys Appearance here wᶜʰ may soone come over to yᵐ Major Stoddard & myself are Secureing all pᵗˢ by scouts & guards as much as we can to pʳvent the Sudden surprizes of the Enemy who doubtless will do all the mischeef they can before they go off with my Humble Service pʳsented to yoʳ Excellency & whole family Rendering my Self   yoʳ   Obeydient & very Humble serᵛᵗ
  Samˡˡ Partridge Yoʳ Excellency's directions is at all tymes advantageous to us[47]

The 'man taken at Springfield' was Benjamin Wright of 'Skipmuck,' and he was

147

Henry R. Stebbins Jr.

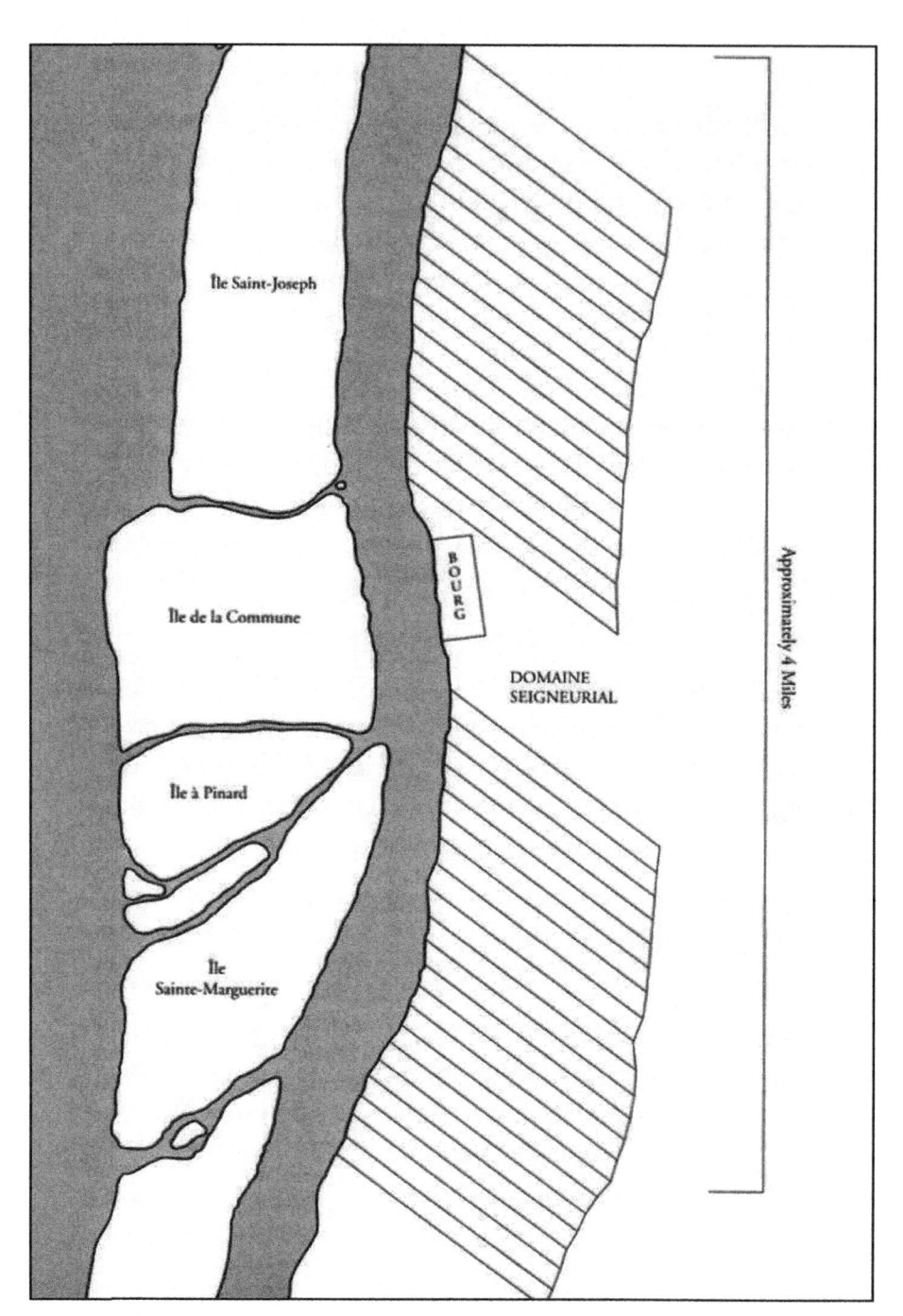

Map 7: Boucherville 1673
(Haefeli & Sweeney 46)

148

The Dead 1704

probably killed soon after. He was 18 years old. The man killed on the western scout was Samuel Andrews of Hartford; the captured men, Benjamin Barrett of Deerfield and Sunderland, and William Sanford, a Connecticut soldier. The party was under the charge of Sergt. Samuel Taylor of Deerfield, who did not keep them under sufficient restraint. They were 'very careless & noisy as they traveled,' says Stephen Williams. Lieut. Samuel Williams was in Canada when the 2 captives were brought in. Both were recovered by him, and brought back in September.[48]

This was a last raid on this valley during Queen Anne's war. The messenger who brought Schuyler's dispatch to Partridge July 31st, said the Governor of Canada expected a speedy peace, but would do as much spoil as he could before it came. It was in continuance of this characteristic and infamous method of carrying on the war, that De Vaudreuil, to make the most of the time, sent a large force against the Eastern towns in September.[49]

A proclamation for the cessation of hostilities was promulgated at Boston October 29th, 1712, and Queen Anne's War was closed by the Treaty of Utrecht, March 30th, 1713.[50]

In this war Deerfield lost 61 killed, 9 wounded and 112 captured. The valley below lost 58 killed, 16 wounded and 13 captured. Total in Hampshire county, 119 killed, 25 wounded, 125 captured.[51]

Settlers taken captive during Queen Anne's War:

Chapter 14

THE AFTERMATH OF QUEEN ANNE'S WAR

Fate of the John Stebbins Jr's Family

Another Deerfield father, John Stebbins, had somewhat better luck. He had watched all of his children carried into captivity among the French. His daughter Abigail's marriage to Jacques de Noyon, which had helped keep them alive and safe in the hands of the French on the march to Canada, had also given them easy entry into Canadian society. Five of John's captive children stayed in Canada after the war; only his son John [III] had returned before the end of the war. John Stebbins Jr. did succeed in enticing his grandson, Aaron de Noyon, to stay when he visited Deerfield, but the boy's mother and four siblings remained in Canada. In an effort to lure them back to New England, Stebbins offered them each in 1723 one-eighth share of his 'lands provided they come and live in New England.' One of the sons, Samuel, responded. He seems to have lived quietly among his siblings in Chambly or Boucherville until about 1728. By then, he was 40. He probably heard of the will's provisions from his sister, Abigail, who visited Deerfield in 1726, but he waited 2 more years – until the Fourth Anglo-Abenaki War had spluttered to an end – before returning to claim his inheritance. By 1731, he was back in New England. He may have been baptized in New France, but there is no evidence that he ever married while living there.[1]

The children of John Stebbins who remained in New France account for many of the captives – and half of the Deerfield males – who entered into French rural life. Unlike most captives, these men were under secular supervision. The Bouchers and Hertels watched over them and set them up on their seigneuries. Ebenezer Stebbins appears to have lived out his life as a farmer in Boucherville. Joseph Stebbins, 4 when captured, set himself at Chambly, where the seigneurie was initially Zachary –

Françoise Hertel who subsequently sold the land to Jean – Baptiste Boucher de Niverville. Joseph married Marguerite James [Gems-Sansoucy] sometime around 1734, when he was in his mid-thirties. Marguerite seems to have been a former captive herself, judging by her surname and the nickname of 'Langlais.' They had 8 children, all but 2 of whom lived to adulthood, just about average for an eighteenth-century habitant family. After Joseph died in 1753, Marguerite remarried [to Jean-Baptiste Menard].[2]

More dramatic support for Joseph's sister, Thankful, came from Joseph – Francois, the Hertel family patriarch. He had taken in Thankful Stebbins as soon as she arrived in Chambly. The Hertels seem to have made sure that she achieved about as much social status as a habitant could. Joseph – Francois and his wife sponsored her baptism and gave her the name Therese. In 1711, when she was 19, she married habitant Charles – Adrien Legrain, called Lavalle. The couple settled in Chambly, where he became a militia captain, the most prominent civil office a habitant could hope to hold. She bore 11 children and died in July 1729, from complications during the birth of her last child. The godparents of her children reveal the network she was able to draw on for support. Claude Hertel de Beaulac and Therese Hertel, wife of Jean – Baptiste Boucher de Niverville, sponsored her first child and the relatives of her brother-in-law Jacques de Noyon sponsored the last child.[3]

While Abigail Stebbins de Noyon's French contacts helped her family out enormously, they did not benefit her much. Jacques de Noyon had seduced Abigail in part with tales of the great amount of property he owned in Canada. But much to her dismay, she 'found nothing not even a home' in new France and had to 'support her family by work of her hands; to lie at the expensive charitable persons, receiving nothing from her husband.' Fortunately for Jacques, French authorities rescinded the death penalty for those who had violated the ban against trade to the Upper Country. Thus, he escaped the ultimate punishment for his earlier actions and departed with a brigade of fur traders almost immediately after their arrival in Canada in April 1704. Subsequently, he became a sergeant. in the *troopes de la marine* in the company of Alphonse de Tonty and probably spent much of his time serving out West with his captain, who was posted to Fort Frontenac and Detroit.[4]

Left on her own in Boucherville, Abigail petitioned for and received a separation of goods so that she could hold property and transact business under her own name. Under the laws of New France, a family's property was regarded as part of a 'marital community' owned equally by both spouses and contracts require the signature of both members of this community. Legal protection was therefore available for wife when a husband's actions threaten to dissipate property that belonged equally to his wife. In New England such protection did not exist because under England's common law a husband legally subsumed his wife in all matters involving the ownership of property. The laws of New France thus gave Abigail and other French women a protection their sisters in New England lacked, though in practice it did little to reduce the patriarchal authority of husbands. The law also made it clear that 'the husband is the master of the [marital] community,' and, as one historian has observed, the protection accorded women such as Abigail 'was the corollary of subjection' to a husband.[5]

This separation of goods involving the De Noyons was not a divorce. Abigail and Jacques continued to have children, and Jacques and his family continued to be involved with the rest of the Canadian Stebbins. It was a business arrangement, one that allowed Abigail, rebaptized as Marguerite in 1708, to conduct real estate transactions on her own, which she did with some success. The arrangement insulated the family's real estate holdings from the vagaries of Jacques's participation in the fur trade and possible spend-thrift ways. As long as Abigail lived, the family did well economically, paying off their mortgage, renting out land, and accumulating some wealth. After she died in 1740, Jacques was unable to add to what Abigail had left him. An inventory of his goods, taken after her death and shortly before his in 1745, reveals his estate was worth less than it had been while she was in charge. He was in debt and everything he had was old and used, acquired by Abigail and never replaced.[6]

Redeemed

John Stebbins, Jr.:

Stebbins, John, son of John of Northampton, born in 1647; was in the Lothrop massacre [Bloody Brook], and is the only man known to escaped unhurt. The second day after, he enlisted under the gallant Capt. Samuel Moseley, and served with him until the close of the war. He remained a few years in the vicinity of Boston, working at the trade of a carpenter. Here he married Dorothy, daughter of John Alexander, a Scotsman, but returned at the Permanent Settlement. In 1704, himself, his wife and five [6] children were captured, and taken to Canada. Three [4] of the younger children never came back. He lived on lot number 35, and died in 1724.[7] John's life closed on Dec. 19, 1724.[8]

In his will he left one-eighth of his lands to each of his children then in Canada, to wit: Samuel, Ebenezer, Joseph, Abigail and Thankful, provided they would come and live in New England. Each one's share, if he died in New England, was to descend to his heirs; otherwise, to revert to those who remained in New England.[9]

> 'Those that will not live in New England', says the old man [John], 'shall have five shillings apiece, and no more.... Yet be it forever understood that if my daughter Abigail come not and tarry as above said, then Aaron Denieur, her son, shall be my Heir in her Room and Stead, provided Said Aaron continue in this Countrey then. After my decease and my wife's decease, Said Aaron shall enter upon that which should have been his mother's part, and possess it until his mother comes, but if She come not and fulfill the above said Conditions, and Aaron stays in New England and doth fulfill them, then the said eighth part of my lands to descend to said Aaron's heirs forever.'.... 'And if some of my children, now in Canada, shall come and fulfill the conditions.... though the rest come not then my lands shall be divided between my son John and Aaron, and those that do come.... John having three times as much as any one of the rest...[10]

Dorothy Stebbins:
Returned to Deerfield.[11]

Samuel:
Samuel, born 1688. Of him we found no Canadian record, nor is he found in New England. In his father's will he is said to be in Canada. Stephen Williams, making a list in 1731 (printed in an appendix of 'The Redeemed Captives,' edition 1853), marks him as having returned.[12] On a trip to Deerfield with his sister Abigail, 'Samuel Stebbins remained in Deerfield'.[13]

John Stebbins [III]:
John was born about 1685. He was captured in 1704, but was redeemed and lived on No. 35 until he died Sept. 7, 1760. Around 1714 he married Mary _____; who

died Aug. 30, 1733 at age 37. On Aug. 25, 1735 he married Hannah, daughter of Edward Allen. She died after John in 1772.

Aaron Denio [De Noyon]:

> The 28 Dec. 1704, I undersigned Priest, cure' of Boucherville, have baptized in the Parish church of the Holy Family, Jacques Rene de Noyon, born on the 26th of the same month and year, of Jacques de Noyon and Gabrielle Stebbin, his wife, living in this parish. His Godfather was Jean Boucher, Sieur de Niverville son of Mr Boucher and godmother was Marie de Boucherville, daughter of Mr de Boucherville, who have signed with me.
>
> Niverville   Marie de Boucherville."[14]

There was much carelessness in the writing of names. In 1710 'Marguerite Stebbens, married to Jean des noyons, sergeant and having children' was naturalized. As Jacques de Noyon was the progenitor of all the Denios of this country it may be well to name some of his forebears.[15]

Aaron [son of Abigail and Jacques de Noyon] when about 10 years old came down with a party of Indians to visit his kin. His grandfather persuaded him to stay, and when the Indians were ready to return, Aaron could not be found. He became a noted tavern keeper in Greenfield, was prominent in public affairs, and a soldier in later years.[16]

It is to be supposed that Jacques and Abigail de Noyon had heard at intervals from their son, and that Rene had informed his mother of his grandfather's death. His uncle John [III] must also have notified his brothers and sisters in Canada of the conditions of their father's will. After much talk, Abigail decided to accompany her brother Samuel to Deerfield. It was certainly no mercenary motive that led her to undertake such a journey under the circumstances. Five shillings was to be her dole if she returned to Canada, and to husband and children she must return. But her heart yearned for the boy from whom she had been separated for years. She longed—who does not? — to revisit the home of her childhood and to see her old mother once more before she died. How or when the journey was performed, how long the visit lasted, and what was her escort on her return to Canada, I know not. I only know that in Deerfield, on the 27th of February, 1726, her thirteenth and last child was born.[17]

Unredeemed

There are many reasons that some members of the John Stebbins, Jr's family decided to take up a permanent residence, *unredeemed*, in Canada. They could have disliked being 'under the ecclesiastical rigor of New England discipline,'[18] or preferred staying with 'the easy-going forms of Catholicism in Canada?'[19] Maybe under the constant Romish pressure they were 'enticed away by some Canadian priest, anxious for [their] soul's salvation?'[20] Did they 'find civilized life uncongenial and irksome, and pining for the primitive freedom of savage customs, steal away into the wilderness for relief?'[21] as did Eunice Williams.[22]

Joseph Stebbins:

He was 4. Neither baptismal nor marriage record has been found, but he *did* marry Marguerite Sanssoucy and lived with her in Chambly where some of their descendants still live.[23]

About 1734 Joseph v Stebbins married Marguerite Sanssoucy.[24]

Their children were Joseph, b. 1735, and m. 1760; Marguerite, b. 1737, m. 1756; Françoise, b. and d. 1741; Marie – Suzanne, b. 1744, m. Claude Benoit at Chambly in 1761, d. 1776; Pierre, b. 1746, who lived to marry; Françoise, b. 1751; Marie-Anne, b. and d. 1753; and Jean-Baptiste, whose baptism we did not find, but who married in 1762 Marie-Joseph Mace according to Tanguay.[25]

Joseph died 'aged 52' the 23 April, 1753, and his widow married Jean-Baptiste Menard. The name Stebbins, in various spellings, is in the Montréal Directory.[26]

A family bearing the name drifted back to the Connecticut Valley and one of them, reading Miss Baker's 'Story of Thankful Stebbins,' questioned his old mother who told him she knew about the captive ancestor.[27]

Joseph is the forefather of my branch of the Stebbins clan, and my great grandfather Henry L. Stebbens *did* return to the Connecticut River Valley as a French-Canadian immigrant in 1902.

Ebenezer Stebbins:

A month after Abigail's baptism father Meriel performed the same rite for him.

> On Friday, June 29th, 1708, I, the undersigned priest baptized an English boy, named in his country Ebenezer Stebbins, who born at Deerfield in New England the – 169 – of the marriage of Jean Stebbins and Dorothee Alexandre both protestants, having been taken 11th February 1704 and brought to Canada, lives in Boucherville with his sister Marguerite Stebbens, wife of Jacques Denoions, Sergeant of the Company of Tonti. He was given the name Jacques Charles. His godfather was M. Jaques Charles de Sabrevoys *Ecuyer Capitaine d'un Detachement de la marine* and his godmother Jeanne Crevier, wife of M. Pierre Boucher *Ecuyer* Seigneur de Boucherville, who have signed with me according to law.   de Sabrevoys Denoyons
>
> Jeanne Crevier, Meriel ptre.[28]

Ebenezer, like John Carter, seems to of been inclined to return to New England for Stoddard wrote '17th May 1714. We sent two men to Bushervil and Point de Tramble, who returned the 18th & informed that Eben Stebbins and John Castor (who so often pretended that they would go home) were not likely to return.' Ebenezer, as Jacques-Charles, had been naturalized in 1710; and of him we know no more.[29]

Abigail De Noyon [Marguerite Denio]:

She was the daughter of John Stebbins, twenty-six days married to James Denio, or Denieur, one of the of "three Frenchmen wars." of Stephen Williams's list, when captured.[30]

In a list of names given by Fitz John Winthrop is 'Denyon, & wife and 2 Frenchman.' Who were these Frenchman and why were they in Deerfield? Two are nameless and doubtless went back to Canada with her countrymen. Miss Baker thought they might have been of the large number of *coureurs de bois*, who were the despair of their government. They carried goods and brandy to the Indians exchanging them for furs. An intendant wrote to Versailles that there was not a family of any condition or quality whatsoever that had not some members engaged in this illicit trade, and the English were ready to profit thereby.[31]

The second son of Jean and Marie was Jacques, baptized at Three Rivers 12 Feb., 1668; and it was he who married Abigail Stebbins. The family had moved to

Boucherville nine miles down the river from Montréal, and there to his own people Jacques took his young bride. For her we may picture a welcome and a home; the only captive for whom such comforts were ready and there her child was born and was sponsored by the seigniorial family.[32]

Abigail had lived 4 years in her Canadian home before she became a Catholic. Then at Montréal:

> On Monday, 28 May 1708, was baptized by me, undersigned Priest, an English woman, named in her own country Abigail Stebbens, who born at Dearfield in New England Jan 4, 1684 of the marriage of Jean Stebbin inhabitant of that place and of Dorothee Alexandre both Protestants, having been baptized by the minister of the place some years after and married the 14th February 1704 to Jacques Desnoiions now Sergeant of Monsieur de Tonty's company, came with him to Canada toward the end of the following March and lives with him at Boucherville. Her name of Abigail has been changed to that of Marguerite. Her godfather was the High and Mighty Seigneur Messire Philippe de Rigault Marquis de Vaudreuil, *Chevalier de l'ordre militaire de Saint Louisshould* and Governor General of New France. Her godmother, Demoiselle Marguerite Bouat, wife of Antoine Pascaut, royal treasury clerk of the Kings revenues in this country, who have signed with me according to the law, Meriel Priest
>
> Marguerite Stebben   Vaudreuil Mgte Bouat Pascaud"[33]

[Note that the careful priest wrote 'came' with her husband. She was not a prisoner! Ebenezer and Thankful were perhaps living with her.[34]]

We have said that for Abigail a home was ready, but a document in the Faillon papers seem to prove the contrary. It is by the notary, 'Pierre Raimbault, Councllor of the King,' and is dated July, 1708, shortly after she was baptized. Literally translated it is:

> "Humbly petitioning, Marguerite Stebe, wife of Jacques de Noyon, English woman, shows that with consent of

her father and mother she had married in her country the said Noyon, who was there at the time; upon his assurance that he would give to her *un etablissment coniderable* and that he possessed much property (*de grande biens*) in this country where she came with him and where, having found nothing not even a home (*pas meme acun asile pour se retirer*) she has been obliged to support her family by the work of her hands; to live at the expense of charitable persons, receiving nothing from her husband and as her work does not suffice to feed her numerous family, she has been advised to purchase land in Boucherville, which is offered at a reasonable price; agreement for payment during a long term being made in her own name which land she hopes to pay for when due (*a constitution de rente en son nom particulier laguelle terre elle espere acquitter le jour par la suite*) both by her heirs and labor as by the help she hopes for from her parents when it shall have pleased God to give us peace…"[35]

Jacques, a soldier, was evidently not a home-maker, and since there was no marriage – contract, as indeed there could have not have been in the New England village, the wife, Abigail – Marguerite by the old French law, as by the present Québec law, 'is held to be common as to the property with her husband,' and she cannot hold anything in her own name, in which case the tribunal may empower her to do so. It is plain that this law made her petition necessary, and here is its answer: 'Marguerite Stebe, accepting for herself her heirs and assigns a grant in the seigniory of Boucherville *en la cote* St. Joseph, of 75 arpents in area [3x25] charged with a seignioral rent of 3 livres 15 sous and 3 live hens. Price 260 livres of the country. Made and passed in Boucherville at the presbytery the 24 August 1708, present Monsieur de la Saudraye and Monsieur Boucher, seigneur,' and further: it is 'Writ which orders the Sieur Pierre-Rodolphe Guibert de la Saudraye, cure of Boucherville to pay Marie Godet, widow of Charles de Couagne, both in her own name and as guardian of her minor children a sum of 500 livres which will constitute a lien and mortgage on the said widow de Couagne's land and house situated at Boucherville, which Pierre Pichette dit Lamusette and his wife Catherine Durant have sold to Marguerite Stebens, wife of Jacques de Noyon by contract of August 24, 1708."[36]

In 1740, November 15, Abigail was buried at Boucherville, age 62, says the record, but only 56 as says the baptismal record. Her husband, "aged about 78," died in 1745[37]

Thankful Stebbins:

She was 12 years old when captured and was probably bought from her Indian master, at Chambly, by some member of the Hertel family. There on one of the first pages of its register is recorded her baptism:[38]

> This 23 of April 1707, I, Pierre Dublaron officiating in the parish of Chambly, certified that I have administered the rite of baptism to louise theresse Stebens, English girl and baptized in england. her godfather and godmother were mre hertelle de chambly and made de perygny, wife of the commandant of the fort of chambly, in faith of which I have signed.[39]

As Therese Stebens she asks for citizenship in 1706. The next year she is godmother for one of Abigail's children at Boucherville. Although married there, the record is on the parish register of Longueil:[40]

> Feb. 4, 1711; After the publication of usual banns made at the mass in the church of the Sainte-Famille at Boucherville on Jan. 25th, Feb. 1st and 2d to which no legal impediment has been found, I, the undersigned priest, cure of Boucherville, have married in the said parish church of Boucherville, Adrien grain, called La Vallee, inhabitant of chambly, aged 23 years, son of deceased Charles le grain and Louyse la fortune living, inhabitant of Chambly with therese louyse Stebens aged 21 years, daughter of Jean Stebens and Dorothee Alexandre his wife, inhabitants of the village of Guiervil in New England, and had given them the nuptial benediction in presence of Joseph Maillot, cousin of the groom, of Sieur Jacques de Noyon, brother-in-law of the bride and others.[41]

Living at Chambly in the Seigniory of Hertel family she seems to have been especially under their patronage.[42]

Below this is written the burial record of the wife of Charles le grain on 11 July, 1729. Close by the Chambly Fort, surrounded by a high picket fence, is the ancient burying ground of the Seigniory. Affixed to the fence-posts of the enclosure are three or four small tablets of wood, bearing the names of French soldiers, and with these is one on which is written:

Terese Stebbins 1729.[43]

Eunice Williams:

Daughter of Rev. John Williams, aged seven. – A full and interesting account of this case can be found in the paper read by Miss C. Alice Baker before the Pocumtuck Valley Memorial Association in 1871. She remained with the Indians until she became practically one of them. Nothing can induce her captors to give her up, either to the English or French. De Vaudreuil says Mr. Williams, her father, 'labored much for her redemption. He offered a hundred pieces of eight for her and was refused. His lady went over and begged her from them, but all in vain.' How shall we account for the tenacity with which the fickle, money-loving savages clung to this child? It was said they 'would as soon part with their hearts,' as with her. Could it have been from personal attachment? Was it not rather through the influence of the Jesuits, plotting a grand triumph over Mr. Williams? Prolonged and earnest efforts were made for her recovery; but when in 1713 she married Amrusus, a Caghnawaga Indian, they were almost as hopeless. In 1740, she was prevailed upon to visit her brother Stephen at Longmeadow, with her husband, on the guarantee that she should not be detained. They came to New England again the next year, with two children, and stayed several months, visiting her relatives; a third time in October, 1743, and once again later. The General Court granted the family a large tract of land on condition they would remain, but to no purpose; she, fearing it would endanger her soul. The only other reason ever given, so far as it appears, was that her father had married a second wife.[44]

As probably the most famous captive, I've included her here. Her well-told story, along with the spiritual/prejudicial strife that her father underwent, is told by him in 'The Redeemed Captive Returning to Zion' by John Williams, Minister of the Gospel in Deerfield.

Chapter 15

SUBSEQUENT DEERFIELD WARS

Father Rasle's War or Drummer's War (1722-1724)

Prior to 1720, tensions increased between the English in New England and the Abenakis in Maine. The English in Maine were encroaching upon territory controlled by the Indians. The English felt justified for two reasons. First, they were ceded this land by the Treaty of Utrecht with the Indian's consent. While they may have consented, the Indians believed that no one truly 'owned' the land and that unrestricted hunting/fishing rights would be theirs forever. Second, the English purchased the land from the Indians by various means. In this instance, Father Rasle in response said that 'an Englishman would give an Indian a bottle of rum, or some article of trifling value, for many acres of land.' This lack of understanding on the part of both parties along with the continued trespassing by the Indians and encroachment by the English created inevitable conflcts.

In the beginning, though the Indians demontrated resentment toward the English advances in many ways, they resisted actual bloodshed. Father Rasle backed these measures, and even threatened more stringent actions because he felt the English were interfering with his missionary work with the Abenakis. Two schools of Abenaki thought developed; those that believed in peace at any price and those that wanted continued resistance. The *peace* group influenced the initial Abenaki actions. In November

1720 they offered to pay reparations for the cattle they killed. They hoped the English would not use military action in response to recent Abenaki *indiscretions* that should have been settled with this offer. In addition, to demonstrate their good intentions, they sent 4 Indians to be held in lieu of the payment.

'Death of Father Sebastian Rasle'
1856
(Maine Memory Network)

The English accepted the payment, but refused to return the hostages. After waiting for a more than reasonable amount of time for the hostage's return, the Abenaki took the law into their own hands and sent a force against Georgetown, driving the English into the fort. With this warlike act, the English proposed to send 2 expeditions against the Indians. It was the second that had as its objective the attack on Norridgewock and the capture of father Rasle. This attempt failed to catch Father Rasle who narrowly escaped with the sacred church vessels in hand.

A declaration of war was made by Governor Shute on July 8, 1722. When he left office on Jan.1 1723 he turned his duties over to Lieutenant-Governor William Drummer. As a result, the war is also known as Drummer's War. He launched an abortive expedition against Norridgewock.

Father Rasle returned to Norridgewock to continue with his religious duties and lending support to the Abenaki. This ended in August 1724 when 4 companies of English surprised the defenders there. The Indians fled leaving Father Rasle to defend himself in a cabin where he was shot and mortally wounded. When they returned, the Indians buried the man that devoted his life to them, and that many thought he was a fearless and resolute hero.

The end of 1724 and the death of John Stebbins, Jr. in December, brings our story to a close. A story told of two brothers, from the first Stebbins generation born in a new land. Men with flaws, yet with their families, were filled with the heroic determination and the raw courage that helped forge the foundation of the new country that had yet to come. Though a lot of negativity surrounds my immediate predecessors, I can't help standing proud, knowing I'm a direct descendant of John and Benoni Stebbins.

French and Indian War or the Old French War (1754-1763)

For Deerfield, now no longer a frontier town, the following war closes the story of its struggle for existence.

With many other names, this war was again the result of a European conflict. Fought primarily between the Colonies, in 1756 the war erupted into a world-wide conflict involving Britain and France with both sides supported by military troops from Europe. The name refers to the two main enemies of the British colonists: the royal French forces and the various Native Americans allied with them. Great Britain also made use of Indian allies.[1]

This far-ranging war covered a large part of the frontier separating New France and the British colonies. It began with a dispute over the confluence of the Allegheny and Monongahela rivers, the site of present-day Pittsburgh. The dispute erupted into violence in the Battle of Jumonville in May 1754, during which Virginia militiamen under the command of George Washington ambushed a French patrol. During 1755 through 1757, British operations in the Pennsyl-

George Washington
Circa 1754

vania New York area failed due to poor management, causing the fall of the British government and the rise of William Pitt. However, in 1755 the British captured a fort resulting in the mass deportation of the Acadians that lived there.[2]

France unwilling to commit sufficient resources to the North American theatre, ultimately lost control of the heartland of New France due to British operations between 1757 and 1760. In the end, Montreal fell to the British in Sept. 1760. France then ceded large tracts of land west of the Mississippi to Spain, thus leaving Britain to dominate the eastern half of North America.

In 1735 Governor Jonathan Belcher of the Province of Massachusetts Bay met with delegates from the six Iroquois Indian Nations at Deerfield, and pledges of friendship were made. At this time, too, services were held in the New Meeting House to ordain John Sergeant as Minister and Missionary to the Housatonic Indians in Stockbridge. Parson Ashley, the successor to Rev. John Williams, whose house is described in this booklet, took part in all the proceedings. Except for intermittent raids and attacks on individuals working their fields, the effects of this peace conference were lasting. The final Indian raid in Deerfield occurred in 1746.[3]

APPENDIXES

Henry R. Stebbins Jr.

APPENDIX A

The Dead 1704

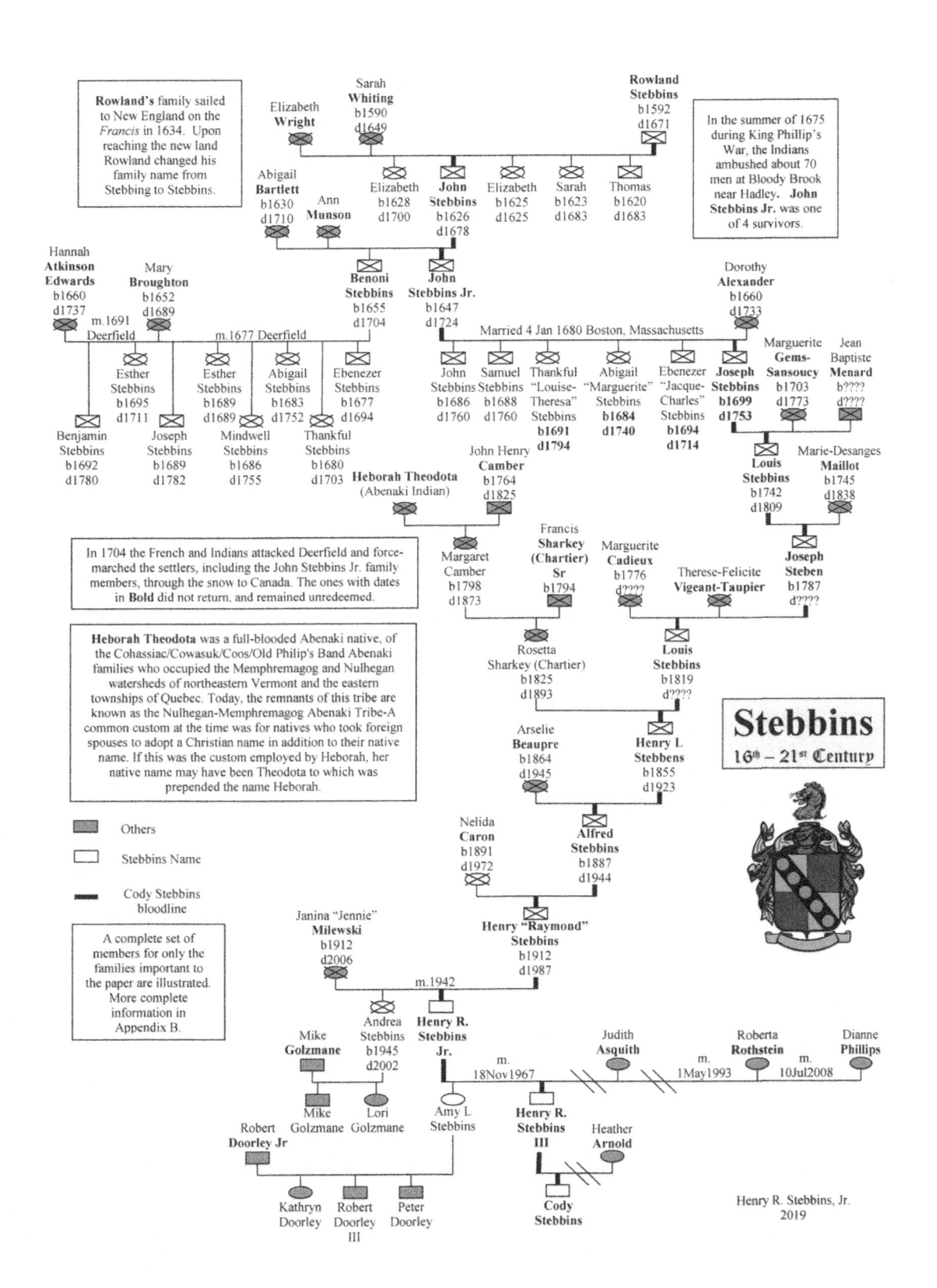

Rowland's family sailed to New England on the *Francis* in 1634. Upon reaching the new land Rowland changed his family name from Stebbing to Stebbins.

In the summer of 1675 during King Phillip's War, the Indians ambushed about 70 men at Bloody Brook near Hadley. **John Stebbins Jr.** was one of 4 survivors.

- Sarah **Whiting** b1590 d1649
- Elizabeth **Wright**
- Rowland **Stebbins** b1592 d1671

Children:
- Abigail **Bartlett** b1630 d1710
- Ann **Munson**
- Elizabeth b1628 d1700
- **John Stebbins** b1626 d1678
- Elizabeth b1625 d1625
- Sarah b1623 d1683
- Thomas b1620 d1683

- Hannah **Atkinson Edwards** b1660 d1737 m.1691 Deerfield
- Mary **Broughton** b1652 d1689 m.1677 Deerfield
- Benoni **Stebbins** b1655 d1704
- **John Stebbins Jr.** b1647 d1724
- Dorothy **Alexander** b1660 d1733

Married 4 Jan 1680 Boston, Massachusetts

Children of John Stebbins Jr. & Dorothy:
- Esther Stebbins b1695 d1711
- Esther Stebbins b1689 d1689
- Abigail Stebbins b1683 d1752
- Ebenezer Stebbins b1677 d1694
- John Stebbins b1686 d1760
- Samuel Stebbins b1688 d1760
- Thankful "Louise-Theresa" Stebbins b1691 d1794
- Abigail "Marguerite" Stebbins b1684 d1740
- Ebenezer "Jacques-Charles" Stebbins b1694 d1714
- **Joseph Stebbins** b1699 d1753
- Marguerite Gems-Sansoucy b1703 d1773
- Jean Baptiste Menard b???? d????

- Benjamin Stebbins b1692 d1780
- Joseph Stebbins b1689 d1782
- Mindwell Stebbins b1686 d1755
- Thankful Stebbins b1680 d1703

Heborah Theodota (Abenaki Indian) — John Henry Camber b1764 d1825

- Louis Stebbins b1742 d1809 — Marie-Desanges Maillot b1745 d1838

In 1704 the French and Indians attacked Deerfield and force-marched the settlers, including the John Stebbins Jr. family members, through the snow to Canada. The ones with dates in **Bold** did not return, and remained unredeemed.

- Margaret Camber b1798 d1873 — Francis Sharkey (Chartier) Sr b1794
- Marguerite Cadieux b1776 d????
- Therese-Felicite Vigeant-Taupier
- Joseph Steben b1787 d????

Heborah Theodota was a full-blooded Abenaki native, of the Cohassiac/Cowasuk/Coos/Old Philip's Band Abenaki families who occupied the Memphremagog and Nulhegan watersheds of northeastern Vermont and the eastern townships of Quebec. Today, the remnants of this tribe are known as the Nulhegan-Memphremagog Abenaki Tribe-A common custom at the time was for natives who took foreign spouses to adopt a Christian name in addition to their native name. If this was the custom employed by Heborah, her native name may have been Theodota to which was prepended the name Heborah.

- Rosetta Sharkey (Chartier) b1825 d1893
- Louis Stebbins b1819 d????

- Arselie Beaupre b1864 d1945 — Henry L Stebbens b1855 d1923

Stebbins 16th – 21st Century

Legend:
- Others
- Stebbins Name
- Cody Stebbins bloodline

A complete set of members for only the families important to the paper are illustrated. More complete information in Appendix B.

- Nelida Caron b1891 d1972 — Alfred Stebbins b1887 d1944

- Janina "Jennie" Milewski b1912 d2006 — Henry "Raymond" Stebbins b1912 d1987 m.1942

- Mike Golzmane — Andrea Stebbins b1945 d2002
- Henry R. Stebbins Jr. m. 18Nov1967
- Judith Asquith m. 1May1993
- Roberta Rothstein m. 10Jul2008
- Dianne Phillips

- Robert Doorley Jr — Mike Golzmane, Lori Golzmane
- Amy L Stebbins — Henry R. Stebbins III — Heather Arnold

- Kathryn Doorley, Robert Doorley III, Peter Doorley
- Cody Stebbins

Henry R. Stebbins, Jr. 2019

169

Henry R. Stebbins Jr.

APPENDIX B

The Dead 1704

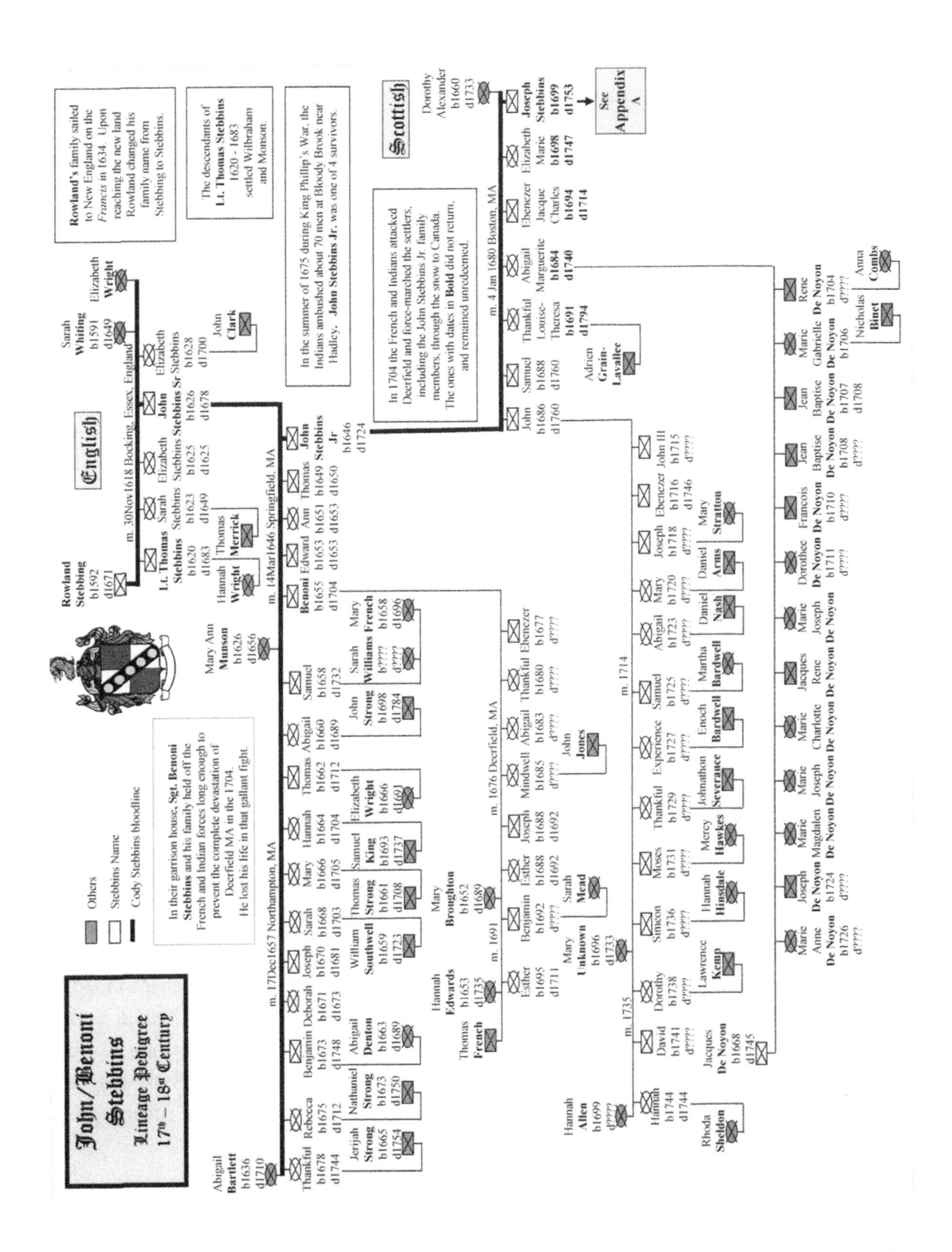

APPENDIX C

New World Generation 1[1]

ROWLAND STEBBINS was born in 1594, in England; died December 14, 1671 (T. R.) at Northampton, MA; married m England to Sarah [WHITING], born, 1591, in England; died October 1649, ["Sarah, wife of Rowland Stebbins, buried 4 (8) 1649." Springfield records at Boston, in New England Historical and Genealogical Register, Vol. 9, p. 171] at Springfield, MA.

CHILDREN:

I. Thomas, b. 1620; m. Hannah WRIGHT
II. Sarah, b. 1623; m. Thomas MERRICK
III. John, b. 1626; m1st Ann [MUNSON]; m2nd Abigail BARTLETT
IV. Elizabeth, b. 1628; m. John CLARK

New World Generation 2[2]

JOHN STEBBINS, son of Rowland Stebbins and Sarah [Whiting], was born 1626, in Ipswich, Suffolk, England; died March 7, 1678 (T. R.) at Northampton, MA; married March 14, 1646, at Springfield, MA, to Ann (MUNSON) MUNDEN. Widow of Abraham Munden. She died in 1656, at Springfield, MA. ["Abraham Munden joyned in marriage to Anne Munson 3rd mon: 16th day 1644." Original record at Springfield, MA. "Nothing more is known of Anne." The Munson Record, Vol. I, page 9.] He married second, December 17, 1657 (T. R.) at Northampton, MA, Abigail BARTLETT, born probably at Hartford, CT, died October10, 1710, at South Hadley Falls, MA, daughter of Robert Bartlett and Anne ____ . Occupation, farmer. Resided at Springfield & Northampton, MA. Widow Abigail (Bartlett) Stebbins married December 28, 1681, (T. R.) Jedediah Strong, son of Elder John Strong.

CHILDREN, born at Springfield, MA:

I.   John, bom January 28, 1647 (T. R.); m. Dorothy ALEXANDER.
II. Thomas, born February 24, 1649; died April 24, 1650 (T.R.)
III. Anna, born April 10, 1651 (T.R.); died October 14, 1653
IV. Edward, born July 12, 1653 (T.R.); died October 14,1653
V.   Benoni, born June 23,1655 (T.R.) m1st Mary (BROUGHTON) BENNETT; m2nd Hannah EDWARDS.

CHILDREN, born at Northampton, MA:

VI.   Samuel, b. January 21, 1658 (T.R.); m. Mary FRENCH
VII.   Abigail, b. May 6, 1660 (T.R.); m. William PHELPS
VIII. Thomas, b. May 6, 1662 (T.R.); m. Elizabeth WRIGHT
IX.   Hannah, b. July 8, 1664 (T.R.); m. John SHELDON
X.   Mary, b. September 10, 1666 (T.R.) m. Thomas STRONG
XI.   Sarah, b. June 4,1668 (T.R.); m. William SOUTHWELL
XII.   Joseph, b. January 17, 1669 (T.R.); died June 3, 1681 (T.R.)
XIII. Deborah, b. March 5, 1671-2 (T.R.); m1st Benjamin ALFORD; m2nd Benjamin BURT
XIV.   Benjamin, b. Mar 3, 1873 in Northampton; died Oct. 12 1778 Belchertown MA[3]
XV.   Rebecca, baptized February 26, 1676; m. Nathaniel STRONG
XVI.   Thankful, b. May 11, 1678; m. Jerijah STRONG

NEW WORLD GENERATION 3[4]

JOHN STEBBINS [Jr.] son of John Stebbins and Anna Munden, was born January 28, 1647, at Springfield, MA; died December 19, 1724 (T. R.) at Deerfield, MA; married about 1683 at Boston MA, to Dorothy ALEXANDER, born 1660, was living at Newton in 1733, who was a daughter of John Alexander and Beartice _____. Occupation, carpenter. Resided at Deerfield, MA.

CHILDREN:

I. John, b. about 1686-7; married 1st, Mary _____; m2nd, Hannah ALLEN
II. Abigail, born January 4, 1684; m. Jaques Deanoions or DE NOYAN
III. Samuel, born December 25, 1688 (T. R.)
IV. Thankful, born September 5, 1691 (T. R.); m. Adrien L. GRAIN-LAVALLEE
V. Ebenezer, born December 5, 1694 (T.R.); remained in Canada
VI. Joseph (or Josiah). Born April 12, 1699 (T. R.); m. Mary SAUSSOUCY
[Entered in the Town Records of Deerfield as Josiah; named in his father's will as Joseph.]
VII. Elizabeth, b.1698, married 29 July, 1715, to Ignace RAIZENNE of the Lake-of-the-Two- Mountains.
[According to the Stebbins Ancestral Society's Message 209: She *was not born to John and Dorothy*. She was also a hostage, and while in route to Quebec her father was killed by the Indians. John and Dorothy took her as his own. There is a lot of confusion her as she was known as Abigail Stebbins, Abigail Nims, Abigail Elizabeth Nims, Elizabeth Stebbins etc. Her real name was Abigail Elizabeth Nims b. 6/11/1700 at Deerfield MA; d. 1/3/1746-7 at Oka Deux, Montagnes, Quebec, Canada. She married Ignace dit Shoentakouani Raizenne on 7/29/1715 at Oka Deux, Montagnes, Quebec, Canada.]

NEW WORLD GENERATION 3 (cont'd.)

BENONI STEBBINS[5] was born June 23, 1655, at Springfield, MA: killed February 29, 1703-4 (T. R.) at Deerfield, MA; married 1676, at Deerfield, MA, to Mary (BROUGHTON) BENNETT, widow of James Bennett, died August 2, 1689 (T. R.) at Deerfield, MA, who was a daughter of John Broughton and Hannah Bascom. He married second, 1691, Hannah EDWARDS widow of Joseph Edwards, died September 7, 1735. Resided at Northampton and Deerfield, MA. Hannah (Edwards) Stebbins, afterwards married Thomas FRENCH.

CHILDREN by Mary Broughton:

I. Ebenezer, b. August 4, 1677; living August 4, 1694.
II. Thankful, b. March 11, 1680 (T. R.)
III. Abigail, b. 1683.
IV. Mindwell, b. January 20, 1685 (T. R.); m. John JONES
V. Joseph, b. February 6, 1688 (T. R.).
VI. Esther, b. February 6, 1688; died January 26, 1690.

CHILDREN by Hannah Edwards:

VII. Benjamin, born September 30, 1692 (T. R.); m. Sarah MEAD.
VIII. Esther, born April 25, 1695 (T. R.); died May 15, 1711 (T. R.).

NEW WORLD GENERATION 4[6]

JOSEPH STEBEN [b. April 12, 1699 in Deerfield], son of John Stebbins and Dorothy, Died April 23, 1753. Alexander marriage contract 18 Nov 1734 before notary Loiseau, Pere. Marguerite SANSOUCY[7]. (She married second, January 25, 1761, Jean-Baptiste Menard, of Chambly.[8,9]

CHILDREN:

I. Joseph, b. Nov. 20, 1735 in Chambly, Quebec; m. 1756; died 21 Apr. 1796 St. Mathias[10,11]
II. Marguerite, b. Sept. 20, 1737 in Chambly; m. 1756; died 1776 in Chambly[12,13]
III. Francoise, b. 1740; died 1741[14]
IV. Jean Baptiste, b. Mar. 22, 1738; m. 5 February. 1762; to Marie-Joseph MACE or MASSE, born 9 July, 1746, dau. of Francois Masse and Madeline Robert.[15,16]
V. Louis Amable, b. 1742 in Chambly; m. 20 Sept. 1773, Chambly to Marie-De sanges MAILLOUX; died Oct 19, 1809[17,18]
VI Marie-Susanne, b. May 31, 1744 in Chambly; m. 26 January 1761, to Claude BENOIT, of Chambly, died 1776.[19,20]
VII. Pierre, b. July 26, 1746 in Chambly; died June 10, 1816.[21,22]
VIII. Francois, b. 11 July, 1751 in Chambly; died July 12, 1751.[23,24]
IX. Marie Anne, b. 25 May, 1753 in Chambly, died 1753.[25,26,27]

JOSEPH STEBBINS was taken captive by the Indians at the destruction of Deerfield, in 1703-4, and was taken by them to Canada. He married in Canada, and settled in Chambly. At the marriage of Dorothee, daughter of Jacques and Abigail Desnoions, at Boucherville, in 1731, JOSEPH STEBBINS was one of the witnesses.

In 1896, two of his descendants were living in Chambly.

NEW WORLD GENERATION 4 (cont'd.)

JOHN STEBBINS III[28] son of John Stebbins and Dorothy Alexander, was born about 1686-7, at Deerfield, MA; died September 7, 1760, at Deerfield, MA; married about 1714, to Mary ____ , born about 1696; died August 30, 1733 (T. R.) at Deerfield, MA. He married second, August (or July) 25, 1735, to Hannah ALLEN, born February 12, 1698-9, daughter of Edward Allen and Mercy Painter. Occupation, farmer. Resided at Deerfield, MA.

CHILDREN, all born at Deerfield:

I. John, b. June 24, 1715 (T. R.) died, unmarried.
II. Ebenezer, b. October 26, 1716 (T. R.); died February 7, 1745-6 (T. R.);
 [probably lost in the Louisburg expedition].
III. Joseph, b. October 20, 1718 (T. R.); m. Mary STRATTON
IV. Mary, b. September 20, 1720 (T. R.); m. Daniel ARMS
V. Abigail, b. March 11, 1723 (T. R.); m. Daniel NASH
VI. Samuel, b. May 5, 1725 (T. R.); m. Martha BARDWELL
VII. Experience, b. October 31, 1727 (T. R.); m. Enoch BARDWELL
VIII. Thankful, b. April 1, 1729 (T, R.); m. Jonathan SEVERANCE
IX. Moses, b. October 18, 1731 (T. R.); m. Mercy HAWKES
X. Simeon, b. August 6, 1736 (T. R.); m. Hannah HINSDALE
XI. Dorothy, b. January 6, 1738 (T. R.); m. Lawrence KEMP
XII. David, b. April 20, 1741; married Rhoda SHELDON
XIII. Hannah, b. February 19, 1744 (T. R.); died June 11, 1744

NEW WORLD GENERATION 4 (cont'd.)

ABIGAIL STEBBINS[29,30] daughter of John Stebbins and Dorothy Alexander, was b. January 4, 1684, at Deerfield. MA: died November 15, 1740, aged 60 years, at Boucherville. Canada: married February 3, 1703 (T. R.) at Deerfield, MA, to Jacques DESNOIONS*, baptised February 12, 1668, at Three Rivers, Canada:

buried May 12, 1745, in Canada, who was a son of Jean Desnoions and Marie Chauvin. Profession, soldier. Religion, Catholic. Residence, Boueherville, Canada.

CHILDREN by the name of Desnoions:

I. Rene (Aaron) Desnoions, b. December 14 (or 26), 1704, in Canada; m. Anna COMBS.
II. Marie Gabrielle Desnoions, b. March 11, 1706: m. Nicholas BINET.
III. Jean Baptiste Desnoions, b. August 11, 1707; died August 11, 1708.
IV. Jean Baptiste Desnoions, b. October 12, 1708.
V. Francois Desnoions, baptised July 7, 1710.
VI. Dorothee Desnoions, b. October 3, 1711.
VII. Marie Joseph Desnoions.
VIII. Jacques Rene Desnoions.
IX. Marie Charlotte Desnoions.
X. Marie Joseph Desnoions.
XI. Marie Magdalen Desnoions.
XII. Joseph Desnoions, b. June 17, 1724.
XIII. Marie Anne Desnoions, b. February 27, 1726, in Deerfield, MA.

* Suddenly, in a most unexpected manner, JACQUES DESNOIONS was restored to his native land. Perhaps his presence on that fateful night of the Deerfield Massacre, Feb. 29, 1704, saved his wife's whole family from the tomahawk. JACQUES DESNOIONS, (or "JAMES DENYO", according to the record of his marriage in Deerfield to "ABIGAIL STEBBINS") and his bride, with her father, mother, brothers, and sisters, were captured and taken to Canada. On a blustering March day in 1704, at the dispersion of the captives at Montreal, JACQUES and his young bride wended their way to his old home at Boucherville. John Stebbins, his wife, Dorothy, and their sons, John and Samuel, returned to Deerfield. ABIGAIL and her husband, her sister Thankfull, and her brothers Ebenezer and Joseph, remained in Canada. On his return to Boucherville, JACQUES probably found his mother and her three youngest children living on the old spot. The surprise with which the family greeted the returned outlaw, with his English bride and her relatives, can well be imagined. Though we may object to the methods of Father Meriel, we cannot but admire his persistent efforts to save the souls of those whom he regarded as heretics.

According to his light, he befriended the captives and there can be no doubt of his sincerity.

THANKFUL STEBBINS[31], daughter of John and Dorothy, Therese Louise (god-daughter of Francois Hartel of Perigny and of Louise De la Valtrie), b. about 1685, in New England; baptized 23 April. 1707. at Chambly; married 4 February, 1711. to Adrien GRAIN-LAVALLEE, at Boucherville.

NEW WORLD GENERATION 5[32,33]

LOUIS [AMABLE] STEBENE, born 1742 in Chambly; son of Joseph Stebbene and Marie-Marguerite Sansouci in Chambly, Quebec, Canada, died October 19, 1809, m. 20 Sept. 1773, Chambly, Quebec, Canada, Marie-Desanges MAILLOUX (MAILHOT), born abt. 1745.

CHILDREN:

I. Louis, b. aft. September 1773, m. June 3, 1793 Marie-Desanges MACE in St. Mathias, Quebec, Canada
II. Joseph, b. aft. September 1773, m1st 21 Nov 1808 Therese VIGNANT in St. Mathias; m2nd Marguerite CADIEUX September 18, 1815 in St. Mathias; died St. Paul de Abbotsford, Quebec
III. Marie-Desanges Stebbins, b. aft. 1774, m. September 24, 1798 Joseph MENNARD in St. Mathias, Quebec, Canada
IV. Marie-Magdalen, b. aft 1774, died November 5, 1779
V. Marie-Therese, b. aft. 1774, December 7, 1780
VI. Marguerite, b. aft. 1774
VII. Toussaint, b. November 13, 1782 in St. Mathias; m. Marie-Elizabeth LALANNE, Marie-Elizabeth MASSE and Josephte MASSELEAU
[one in Sep. 25, 1803 in St. Mathias, Quebec, Canada]
VIII. Marguerite, b. abt. 1792, died bef. September 9, 1835, m. August 17, 1812 Louis VIGNANT in St. Mathias, Quebec, Canada.

NEW WORLD GENERATION 6[34,35,36]

JOSEPH STEBEN, b. aft. September 1773 son of Louis Stebbene and Desanges Mailloux, died St. Paul de Abbotsford, Quebec, Canada, m. 18 Sept. 1815, St. Mathias, Quebec, Canada Marguerite CADIEUX, born abt. 1776 St. Paul de Abbotsford, Quebec, Canada. (Note: He was the widower of Therese-Felicite VIGNANT-TAUPIER, whom he had married 21 Nov 1808, also in St. Mathias.) Joseph Stebbins was at the Battle of Plattsburgh, in 1812, being with the British Army. Occupation joiner. Politics, Liberal. Religion, Catholic

CHILDREN with Therese:

I.   Joseph, b. aft. 1808

CHILDREN with Marguerite:

II.   Joseph, b. aft. 1816
III. Timothy, b. aft. 1816
IV.   Pierre, b. abt. 1817; m. October 25, 1842 Marguerite James-SANSOUCY in St. Pierre, Quebec, Canada
V.   Louis, b. October 13, 1819; m. Rosetta SHARKEY.
VI.   Marguerite, b. abt. 1823, m. November 8, 1842 Jean-Baptiste PION in St. Pierre, Quebec, Canada
VII   Adeline, b. abt. 1823; m. October 24, 1843 Etienne Benjamin ST. AUBIN in St. Pie, Quebec, Canada
VIII. Marie-Madeline, b. abt. 1837; m. July 20, 1857 Moise BEAUDRY in St. Pierre, Quebec, Canada

NEW WORLD GENERATION 7[37,38]

LEWIS STEBBINS, son of Joseph Stebbins and Margaret Cadieux, was b. October 13, 1819, at St. Mathias, Province Quebec; married October 23, 1849. Rosetts SHARKEY[36], born July 8, 1825, who was the daughter of Francis Sharkey and Maryette Camber. Occupation, farmer. Politics, Liberal. Residence, Abbotsford,

Province Quebec. Lewis Stebbins worked as a millwright in New York state for several years.

CHILDREN:

I. Francis, b. August 1850; died January 5, 1854.
II. Mary A., b. July 21, 1852; m. Joseph DUFRESNE.
III. Henry L., b. May 1, 1855; m. Arzalie BAUPREE[39]
IV. Adeline E., b. September 25, 1857; m. William LUCIER.
V. Rosina M., b. December 18, 1859; m. Octave LAROSE
VI. Julia V., b. November 16, 1862; m. Pierre MONNARD.
VII. Joseph, b. June 5, 1865; m. Emilia BRILLON.
VIII. Arthur, b. June 18, 1868; died April 5, 1869.
IX. Emma, b. July 3, 1872; m. Delphis CHOINIEL.

NEW WORLD GENERATION 8[40]

HENRY L. STEBBENS born 1 May 1855 Quebec, son of Lewis Stebbins and Rosetta Sharkey (Chartier), married 9 Feb 1879 Arzalie BAUPREE (born 1864, died 1945) in Valcourt, Shefford, Quebec, Canada. Died 1923. Occupation: farmer. Immigrated to the USA in 1902 at age 46.

CHILDREN:

I. Emma 1880-1957; m. Paul Suzor,
II. Sr. Marie-Agnes 1882-1972; nun
III. Loria 1883-1944
IV. Joseph 1885-1937; m. Olive Lamothe
V. Alfred 1887-1944; m. Nelida Caron
VI. Theodore 1889-1975; m. Etinette Lemieux
VII. Cora 1893-1959; m. Phillip Boyer
VIII. Emil 1890-1954; m. Lelea Gaudreau
IX. Anna 1894-1963; m. Felix Larose
X. Robert 1896-1974; m. Loretta Mae Duquette

XI. Grace 1897-1976; m. John Roy
XII. Rouville/Adelard 1899-1904
XIII. Yvonne 1902-1905
XIV. Athanase 1904-1975; m. Marie Y St. Marie
XV. Marie-Rose 1906-1995; m. Joseph Roy
XVI. Bernadette 1908-2001; m1. Albert Tompkins, m2. William Aker

NEW WORLD GENERATION 9[41]

ALFRED STEBBINS born 24 Jun 1887 in St. Paul, Quebec, Canada; son of Henry L. Stebbens and Arzalie Baupree, married 28 Jun 1909 Nelida CARON (born abt. 1890). Occupation: machinist carpet mill. Immigrated to the USA in 1902 abt. Age 13.

CHILDREN:

I. Roland, born in 1911-1955 in Springfield MA; m. Madeline LAROCHE
II. Henry R. 1912-1987; m. Jennie MILEWSKI
III. Harold 1914-1977
IV. Dorothy 1920-2001; m. Paul JURKOWSKI
V. Robert 1917-1984
VI. Donald 1926-1988
VII. Anita 1931-?; m. Jim GUINN

NEW WORLD GENERATION 10[42]

HENRY "RAYMOND" LOUIS STEBBINS born 12 Jan 1912, son of Alfred Stebbins and Nelida Caron, married Jennie MILEWSKI on 1942. Occupation: auto mechanic. Jennie received a degree from Bay Path in accounting. She died in Springfield MA.

CHILDREN:

Henry R. Stebbins Jr.

I. Henry R. Jr., *living*
II. Andrea L. 1945-2002; m. Michael GOLZMANE

NEW WORLD GENERATION 11[43]

HENRY R. STEBBINS JR., *living,* born in Ludlow MA, son of Raymond Stebbins and Jennie MILEWSKI, married first on 18 Nov 1967 Judith ASQUITH in Wilbraham MA, married second on 1 May 1993 Roberta ROTHSTEIN in Westerly RI, married third on 10 Jul 2008 Dianne (PHILLIPS) IDE/ALLAIRE in Westerly RI, graduate of Michigan State University and Eastern Connecticut University. Occupations: physics/chemistry teacher and roofer.

CHILDREN:

I. Amy L., *living,* born in Westerly, married Robert DOORLEY in Westerly RI. Occupation: Nurse Practitioner
II. Henry R III, *living,* born in Westerly RI

NEW WORLD GENERATION 12[44]

HENRY R. STEBBINS III, *living,* born in Westerly, son of Henry R. Stebbins Jr. and Judith ASQUITH. Occupation: CNA, Phlebotomist

CHILDREN:

I. CODY, *living,* son of Henry R Stebbins III and Heather ARNOLD

ENDNOTES

INTRODUCTION

1   Sheldon, George. *A History of Deerfield Massachusetts: The Times When and The People by Whom It Was Settled, Unsettled and Resettled,* Deerfield, Mass: Pocumtuck Valley Memorial Association, Reprint 2004, Vol.1:9

JUVENILE DELINQUENTS

1   Greenlee, Ralph Stebbins and Greenlee, Robert Lemuel. *The Stebbins Genealogy, Volumes 1&2,* Chicago Illinois, Printed Privately, 1904 (reprinted on CD), 103-104

2   Ibid., pg. 108

3   Baker, C. Alice. *True Stories of New England Captives Carried to Canada during the Old French and Indian Wars.* Westminster MD: Heritage Books Inc., Reprint 2007, 227-228

4   Ibid., 229-230

5   Ibid., 230

6   Melvoin, Richard I. *New England Outpost: War and Society in Colonial Deerfield.* New York: W. W. Norton & Company, 1989, 82

KING PHILIP'S WAR

1   Historic Deerfield, Inc. *A Brief History of Deerfield Massachusetts*. Old Deerfield, Mass: 1972, 3-4
2   Tougias, Michael. "King Philip's War in New England, (America's First Major Indian War)" *The History Place*. 1997: 10 Sept.2000 <http://www.historyplace.com/ specials/ calendar/ docs-pix/aug-kingphilip.htm>
3   Bourne, Russell. *The Red Kings Rebellion: Racial Politics in New England 1675-1678*. Atheneum, Macmillan Publishing Company, 1990, 12
4   Ibid., xiv
5   Ibid., 6-7
6   Ibid., 4
7   Ibid., 8
8   Ibid. 26-27
9   Ibid., 12
10 Ibid., 26
11 Ibid., 26
12 Ibid., 27
13 Ibid., 28
14 Ibid., 132
15 Ibid., 135
16 Ibid., 2-3
17 Ibid., 3
18 Ibid., 133-134
19 Ibid., 134
20 Ibid., 136
21 Ibid., 136-137
22 Ibid., 137
23 Ibid. 137
24 Ibid., 138
25 Ibid., 139
26 Ibid., 141 27
27 Ibid., 141
28 Melvoin, Richard I. *New England Outpost: War and Society in Colonial Deerfield*. New York: W. W. Norton & Company, 1989, 102
29 Sheldon, George. *A History of Deerfield Massachusetts: The Times When and The People by Whom It Was Settled, Unsettled and Resettled,* Deerfield,

Mass: Pocumtuck Valley Memorial Association, Reprint 2004, Vol. 1: 100-102

30   Bourne, Russell. *The Red Kings Rebellion: Racial Politics in New England 1675-1678.* Atheneum, Macmillan Publishing Company, 1990, 132

31   Sheldon, George. *A History of Deerfield Massachusetts: The Times When and The People by Whom It Was Settled, Unsettled and Resettled,* Deerfield, Mass: Pocumtuck Valley Memorial Association, Reprint 2004, Vol. 1: 100-102

32   Baker, C. Alice. *True Stories of New England Captives Carried to Canada during the Old French and Indian Wars.* Westminster MD: Heritage Books Inc., Reprint 2007, 100

33   Sheldon, George. *A History of Deerfield Massachusetts: The Times When and The People by Whom It Was Settled, Unsettled and Resettled*, Deerfield, Mass: Pocumtuck Valley Memorial Association, Reprint 2004, Vol. 1: 102

34   Bourne, Russell. *The Red Kings Rebellion: Racial Politics in New England 1675-1678.* Atheneum, Macmillan Publishing Company, 1990, 142-143

35   Sheldon, George. *A History of Deerfield Massachusetts: The Times When and The People by Whom It Was Settled, Unsettled and Resettled*, Deerfield, Mass: Pocumtuck Valley Memorial Association, Reprint 2004, Vol. 1: 102

36   Melvoin, Richard I. *New England Outpost: War and Society in Colonial Deerfield.* New York: W. W. Norton & Company, 1989, 103

37   Baker, C. Alice. *True Stories of New England Captives Carried to Canada during the Old French and Indian Wars.* Westminster MD: Heritage Books Inc., Reprint 2007, 259

38   Sheldon, George. *A History of Deerfield Massachusetts: The Times When and The People by Whom It Was Settled, Unsettled and Resettled,* Deerfield, Mass: Pocumtuck Valley Memorial Association, Reprint 2004, Vol. 1: 109

39   Greenlee, Ralph Stebbins and Greenlee, Robert Lemuel. *The Stebbins Genealogy, Volumes 1&2,* Chicago Illinois, Printed Privately, 1904 (reprinted on CD), 104

40   Tougias, Michael. "King Philip's War in New England, (America's First Major Indian War)" *The History Place.* 1997: 10 Sept.2000 http://www.histo ryplace.com/specials calendar/docs-pix/aug-kingphilip.htm

41   Haefeli, Evan and Sweeney, Kevin. *Captors and Captives: The 1704 French And Indian Raid on Deerfield.* Amherst Mass: University of Massachusetts

Press, 2003, 23-24
42 Baker, C. Alice. *True Stories of New England Captives Carried to Canada during the Old French and Indian Wars.* Westminster MD: Heritage Books Inc., Reprint 2007, 231
43 Haefeli, Evan and Sweeney, Kevin. *Captors and Captives: The 1704 French And Indian Raid on Deerfield.* Amherst Mass: University of Massachusetts Press, 2003, 21-22
44 Coleman, Emma L. *New England Captives Carried to Canada,* Westminster MD, Heritage Books, Reprint 2008 Vol. 1:132
45 Baker, C. Alice. *True Stories of New England Captives Carried to Canada during the Old French and Indian Wars.* Westminster MD: Heritage Books Inc., Reprint 2007, 116
46 Coleman, Emma L. *New England Captives Carried to Canada,* Westminster MD, Heritage Books, Reprint 2008, Vol. 2:33
47 Ibid., Vol. 1:132
48 Melvoin, Richard I. *New England Outpost: War and Society in Colonial Deerfield.* New York: W. W. Norton & Company, 1989, 124-125

THE STRANGE DEATH OF JOHN STEBBINS, SENIOR

1 Greenlee, Ralph Stebbins and Greenlee, Robert Lemuel. *The Stebbins Genealogy, Volumes 1&2.* Chicago Illinois, Printed Privately, 1904 (reprinted on CD) 77

PERMANENT SETTLEMENT

1 Haefeli, Evan and Sweeney, Kevin. *Captors and Captives: The 1704 French And Indian Raid on Deerfield.* Amherst Mass: University of Massachusetts Press, 2003, 24
2 Baker, C. Alice. *True Stories of New England Captives Carried to Canada during the Old French and Indian Wars.* Westminster MD: Heritage Books Inc., Reprint 2007, 233
3 Sheldon, George. *A History of Deerfield Massachusetts: The Times When and The People by Whom It Was Settled, Unsettled and Resettled,* Deerfield,

Mass: Pocumtuck Valley Memorial Association, Reprint 2004, Vol. 1:190-191
4. Ibid., Vol. 1:193
5. Baker, C. Alice. *True Stories of New England Captives Carried to Canada during the Old French and Indian Wars.* Westminster MD: Heritage Books Inc., Reprint 2007, 161
6. Melvoin, Richard I. *New England Outpost: War and Society in Colonial Deerfield.* New York: W. W. Norton & Company, 1989, 138
7. Sheldon, George. *A History of Deerfield Massachusetts: The Times When and The People by Whom It Was Settled, Unsettled and Resettled.* Deerfield, Mass: Pocumtuck Valley Memorial Association, Reprint 2004, Vol. 1:47
8. Ibid., Vol. 1:216
9. Melvoin, Richard I. *New England Outpost: War and Society in Colonial Deerfield.* New York: W. W. Norton & Company, 1989, 170
10. Coleman, Emma L. *New England Captives Carried to Canada,* Westminster MD, Heritage Books, Reprint 2008, Vol. 2:33
11. Haefeli, Evan and Sweeney, Kevin. *Captors and Captives: The 1704 French And Indian Raid on Deerfield.* Amherst Mass: University of Massachusetts Press, 2003, 24
12. Haefeli, Evan and Sweeney, Kevin. *Captors and Captives: The 1704 French And Indian Raid on Deerfield.* Amherst Mass: University of Massachusetts Press, 2003, 22
13. Ibid., 23
14. Ibid., 24
15. Ibid., 26
16. Ibid., 27
17. Sheldon, George. *A History of Deerfield Massachusetts: The Times When and The People by Whom It Was Settled, Unsettled and Resettled,* Deerfield, Mass: Pocumtuck Valley Memorial Association, Reprint 2004, Vol. 1:206)
18. Ibid., Vol. 1: 212
19. Ibid., Vol. 1: 211-212
20. Melvoin, Richard I. *New England Outpost: War and Society in Colonial Deerfield.* New York: W. W. Norton & Company, 1989, 185
21. Greenlee, Ralph Stebbins and Greenlee, Robert Lemuel. *The Stebbins Genealogy, Volumes 1&2.* Chicago Illinois, Printed Privately, 1904 (reprinted

on CD) 114

KING WILLIAM'S WAR

1. *King Williams War.* Wikipedia Http://en.wikipedia.org/wiki/King_William%27s_War

2. Baker, C. Alice. *True Stories of New England Captives Carried to Canada during the Old French and Indian Wars.* Westminster MD: Heritage Books Inc., Reprint 2007, 162

3. Sheldon, George. *A History of Deerfield Massachusetts: The Times When and The People by Whom It Was Settled, Unsettled and Resettled,* Deerfield, Mass: Pocumtuck Valley Memorial Association, Reprint 2004, Vol. 1: 227

4. Ibid., Vol. 1:202

5. Ibid., Vol. 1:273

THE SARAH SMITH AFFAIR

1. Melvoin, Richard I. *New England Outpost: War and Society in Colonial Deerfield.* New York: W. W. Norton & Company, 1989, 204

2. Ibid., 204-205

3. Ibid., 205

4. Ibid., 205-207

QUEEN ANNE'S WAR: The War of Spanish Succession

1. Greenlee, Ralph Stebbins and Greenlee, Robert Lemuel. *The Stebbins Genealogy, Volumes 1&2.* Chicago Illinois, Printed Privately, 1904 (reprinted on CD) 105

2. Melvoin, Richard I. *New England Outpost: War and Society in Colonial Deerfield.* New York: W. W. Norton & Company, 1989, 209

3. Ibid., 209

4. Ibid., 209

5 Sheldon, George. *A History of Deerfield Massachusetts: The Times When and The People by Whom It Was Settled, Unsettled And Resettled.* Deerfield, Mass: Pocumtuck Valley Memorial Association, Reprint 2004, Vol. 1:283

6 Haefeli, Evan and Sweeney, Kevin. *Captors and Captives: The 1704 French And Indian Raid on Deerfield.* Amherst Mass: University of Massachusetts Press, 2003, 1-2

7 Sheldon, George. *A History of Deerfield Massachusetts: The Times When and The People by Whom It Was Settled, Unsettled and Resettled.* Deerfield, Mass: Pocumtuck Valley Memorial Association, Reprint 2004, Vol. 1:284

8 Melvoin, Richard I. *New England Outpost: War and Society in Colonial Deerfield.* New York: W. W. Norton & Company, 1989, 210

9 Haefeli, Evan and Sweeney, Kevin. *Captors and Captives: The 1704 French And Indian Raid on Deerfield.* Amherst Mass: University of Massachusetts Press, 2003, 2

10 Calloway, Colin G. *The Western Abenakis of Vermont, 1600-1800.* University of Oklahoma Press, Norman Publishing Division of the University, 1994, 15

11 Sheldon, George. *A History of Deerfield Massachusetts: The Times When and The People by Whom It Was Settled, Unsettled and Resettled.* Deerfield, Mass: Pocumtuck Valley Memorial Association, Reprint 2004, Vol. 1:293

12 Ibid., Vol. 1:294

13 Ibid., Vol. 1:294

14 Ibid., Vol. 1:294

15 Ibid., Vol. 1:294

16 Melvoin, Richard I. *New England Outpost: War and Society in Colonial Deerfield.* New York: W. W. Norton & Company, 1989, 211

17 Sheldon, George. *A History of Deerfield Massachusetts: The Times When and The People by Whom It Was Settled, Unsettled and Resettled.* Deerfield, Mass: Pocumtuck Valley Memorial Association, Reprint 2004, Vol. 1:283-284

18 Ibid., Vol. 1:284

19 Melvoin, Richard I. *New England Outpost: War and Society in Colonial Deerfield.* New York: W. W. Norton & Company, 1989, 211

20 Sheldon, George. *A History of Deerfield Massachusetts: The Times When and The People by Whom It Was Settled, Unsettled and Resettled.* Deerfield, Mass: Pocumtuck Valley Memorial Association, Reprint 2004, Vol. 1:284

21   Ibid., Vol. 1:284-285
22   Melvoin, Richard I. *New England Outpost: War and Society in Colonial Deerfield.* New York: W. W. Norton & Company, 1989, 211-212
23   Ibid., 213
24   Ibid., 214
25   Sheldon, George. *A History of Deerfield Massachusetts: The Times When and The People by Whom It Was Settled, Unsettled and Resettled.* Deerfield, Mass: Pocumtuck Valley Memorial Association, Reprint 2004, Vol. 1:287
26   Ibid., Sheldon, Vol. 1:287-288
27   Melvoin, Richard I. *New England Outpost: War and Society in Colonial Deerfield.* New York: W. W. Norton & Company, 1989, 214
28   Sheldon, George. *A History of Deerfield Massachusetts: The Times When and The People by Whom It Was Settled, Unsettled and Resettled.* Deerfield, Mass: Pocumtuck Valley Memorial Association, Reprint 2004, Vol. 1:287
29   Vol. 1:290-291
30   Ibid., Vol. 1:288
31   Melvoin, Richard I. *New England Outpost: War and Society in Colonial Deerfield.* New York: W. W. Norton & Company, 1989, 215
32   Sheldon, George. *A History of Deerfield Massachusetts: The Times When and The People by Whom It Was Settled, Unsettled and Resettled.* Deerfield, Mass: Pocumtuck Valley Memorial Association, Reprint 2004, Vol. 1:288
33   Ibid., Vol. 1:290
34   Ibid., Vol. 1:290-291
35   Ibid., Vol. 1:291-292
36   Ibid., Vol. 1:292
37   Melvoin, Richard I. *New England Outpost: War and Society in Colonial Deerfield.* New York: W. W. Norton & Company, 1989, 215
38   Haefeli, Evan and Sweeney, Kevin. *Captors and Captives: The 1704 French And Indian Raid on Deerfield.* Amherst Mass: University of Massachusetts Press, 2003, 106
39   bid., 106
40   Ibid., 106-107
41   Ibid., 107-108
42   Ibid., 108
43   Greenlee, Ralph Stebbins and Greenlee, Robert Lemuel. *The Stebbins*

Genealogy, Volumes 1&2. Chicago Illinois, Printed Privately, 1904 (reprinted on CD), 161

44 Baker, C. Alice. *True Stories of New England Captives Carried to Canada during the Old French and Indian Wars.* Westminster MD: Heritage Books Inc., Reprint 2007, 206-207

45 Haefeli, Evan and Sweeney, Kevin. *Captors and Captives: The 1704 French And Indian Raid on Deerfield.* Amherst Mass: University of Massachusetts Press, 2003, 108-109

46 Ibid., 109

47 Baker, C. Alice. *True Stories of New England Captives Carried to Canada during the Old French and Indian Wars.* Westminster MD: Heritage Books Inc., Reprint 2007, 217

48 Melvoin, Richard I. *New England Outpost: War and Society in Colonial Deerfield.* New York: W. W. Norton & Company, 1989, 215-216

49 Ibid., 216

50 Ibid., 216

51 Ibid., 216

52 Sheldon, George. *A History of Deerfield Massachusetts: The Times When and The People by Whom It Was Settled, Unsettled and Resettled.* Deerfield, Mass: Pocumtuck Valley Memorial Association, Reprint 2004, Vol. 1:292-293

53 Ibid., Vol. 1:293

54 Melvoin, Richard I. *New England Outpost: War and Society in Colonial Deerfield.* New York: W. W. Norton & Company, 1989, 216-217

55 Sheldon, George. *A History of Deerfield Massachusetts: The Times When and The People by Whom It Was Settled, Unsettled and Resettled.* Deerfield, Mass: Pocumtuck Valley Memorial Association, Reprint 2004, Vol. 1:294

56 Ibid., Vol. 1:295

DEERFIELD: Raid or Massacre?

1 Haefeli, Evan and Sweeney, Kevin. *Captors and Captives: The 1704 French And Indian Raid on Deerfield.* Amherst Mass: University of Massachusetts Press, 2003, 112

2   Ibid., 112
3   Ibid., 112
4   Ibid., 112-113
5   Ibid., 113
6   Ibid., 113
7   Ibid., 113-115
8   Ibid., 115
9   Ibid., 115
10 Ibid., 115-116
11 Ibid., 116
12 Ibid., 116
13 Ibid., 116-117
14 Ibid., 117
15 Ibid., 117
16 Baker, C. Alice. *True Stories of New England Captives Carried to Canada during the Old French and Indian Wars.* Westminster MD: Heritage Books Inc., Reprint 2007, 167
17 Haefeli, Evan and Sweeney, Kevin. *Captors and Captives: The 1704 French And Indian Raid on Deerfield.* Amherst Mass: University of Massachusetts Press, 2003, 117-118
18 Ibid., 118-119
19 Baker, C. Alice. *True Stories of New England Captives Carried to Canada during the Old French and Indian Wars.* Westminster MD: Heritage Books Inc., Reprint 2007, 235
20 Sheldon, George. *A History of Deerfield Massachusetts: The Times When and The People by Whom It Was Settled, Unsettled and Resettled.* Deerfield, Mass: Pocumtuck Valley Memorial Association, Reprint 2004, Vol. 1:314
21 Haefeli, Evan and Sweeney, Kevin. *Captors and Captives: The 1704 French And Indian Raid on Deerfield.* Amherst Mass: University of Massachusetts Press, 2003, 117
22 Ibid., 119
23 Ibid., 117
24 Ibid., 119
25 Ibid., 119-120
26 Ibid., 120

27   Ibid, 120
28   Ibid., 120
29   Ibid., 120-121
30   Ibid., 121-122
31   Ibid., 122
32   Ibid., 122
33   Ibid., 122
34   Ibid., 123
35   Ibid., 123
36   Ibid., 123-124
37   Ibid., 124
38   Ibid., 124

ADDITIONAL NOTES ON THE BATTLE

1   Sheldon, George. *A History of Deerfield Massachusetts: The Times When and The People by Whom It Was Settled, Unsettled and Resettled.* Deerfield, Mass: Pocumtuck Valley Memorial Association, Reprint 2004, Vol. 1:307
2   Ibid., Vol. 1:309-310
3   Ibid., Vol. 1:311-312
4   Ibid., Vol. 1:313
5   Baker, C. Alice. *True Stories of New England Captives Carried to Canada during the Old French and Indian Wars.* Westminster MD: Heritage Books Inc., Reprint 2007, 274
6   Drake, Samuel A. *The Border Wars of New England.* Williamstown MA, Corner House Publishers, 1973, 180-181
7   Williams, John. *The Redeemed Captive Returning to Zion.* Bedford MA, Applewood Books, Reprint 1853, 11

FORCED MARCH INTO CAPTIVITY

1   Haefeli, Evan and Sweeney, Kevin. *Captors and Captives: The 1704 French And Indian Raid on Deerfield.* Amherst Mass: University of Massachusetts Press, 2003, 125

2   Ibid., 125
3   Ibid., 125-126
4   Ibid., 126
5   Ibid., 126-127
6   Ibid., 127
7   Ibid., 132-133
8   Sheldon, George. *A History of Deerfield Massachusetts: The Times When and The People by Whom It Was Settled, Unsettled and Resettled.* Deerfield, Mass: Pocumtuck Valley Memorial Association, Reprint 2004, Vol. 1:315-316
9   Ibid., Vol. 1:316
10 Ibid., Vol. 1:316
11 Coleman, Emma L. *New England Captives Carried to Canada,* Westminster MD, Heritage Books, Reprint 2008, Vol. 1:124-125
12 Coleman, Emma L. *New England Captives Carried to Canada,* Westminster MD, Heritage Books, Reprint 2008, Vol. 1:125
13 Ibid., Vol. 1:125
14 Ibid., Vol. 1:125-128
15 Ibid., Vol. 1:128

POST BATTLE FALLOUT

1   McDonald, Heather. *Interview.* St. Regis Mohawk Reservation. 2012
2   Sheldon, George. *A History of Deerfield Massachusetts: The Times When and The People by Whom It Was Settled, UnsettledaAnd Resettled.* Deerfield, Mass: Pocumtuck Valley Memorial Association, Reprint 2004, Vol. 1:298
3   Ibid., Vol. 1:298
4   Ibid., Vol. 1:300
5   Ibid., Vol. 1:300
6   Ibid., Vol. 1:306
7   Ibid., Vol. 1:306
8   Ibid., Vol. 1:306
9   Ibid., Vol. 1:306-307
10 Ibid., Vol. 1:307

11   Ibid., Vol. 1:304
12   Ibid., Vol. 1:308
13   Ibid., Vol. 1:309
14   Ibid., Vol. 1:316-317
15   Ibid., Vol. 1:7-8
16   Penhallow, Samuel. *History of the Indian Wars.* Williamstown MA, Corner House Publishers, 1973 reprint
17   Coleman, Emma L. *New England Captives Carried to Canada,* Westminster MD, Heritage Books, Reprint 2008, Vol. 1:8-9
18   Sheldon, George. *A History of Deerfield Massachusetts: The Times When and The People by Whom It Was Settled, Unsettled and Resettled.* Deerfield, Mass: Pocumtuck Valley Memorial Association, Reprint 2004, Vol. 1:317
19   Ibid., Vol. 1:317
20   Ibid., Vol. 1:317-318
21   Ibid., Vol. 1:318
22   Ibid., Vol. 1:318
23   Ibid., Vol. 1:318
24   Ibid., Vol. 1:318-319
25   Ibid., Vol. 1:319
26   Ibid., Vol. 1:319
27   Ibid., Vol. 1:319
28   Ibid., Vol. 1:319-320
29   Ibid., Vol. 1:320
30   Ibid., Vol. 1:320
31   Ibid., Vol. 1:320
32   Ibid., Vol. 1:320
33   Ibid., Vol. 1:320-321
34   Ibid., Vol. 1:321
35   Ibid., Vol. 1:321-322
36   Ibid., Vol. 1:322
37   Ibid., Vol. 1:322
38   Ibid., Vol. 1:322
39   Ibid., Vol. 1:322

REDEMPTION OF CAPTIVES

1. Sheldon, George. *A History of Deerfield Massachusetts: The Times When and The People by Whom It Was Settled, Unsettled and Resettled.* Deerfield, Mass: Pocumtuck Valley Memorial Association, Reprint 2004, Vol. 1:324-325
2. Ibid., Vol. 1:325-326
3. Ibid., Vol. 1:326
4. Ibid., Vol. 1:326
5. Ibid., Vol. 1:326-327
6. Ibid., Vol. 1:327
7. Ibid., Vol. 1:328
8. Ibid., Vol. 1:328-329
9. Ibid., Vol. 1:329
10. Ibid., Vol. 1:329
11. Ibid., Vol. 1:330
12. Ibid., Vol. 1:330
13. Ibid., Vol. 1:330
14. Ibid., Vol. 1:332
15. Ibid., Vol. 1:332
16. Ibid., Vol. 1:332
17. Ibid., Vol. 1:332-333
18. Ibid., Vol. 1:333
19. Ibid., Vol. 1:333
20. Ibid., Vol. 1:333
21. Ibid., Vol. 1:333-334
22. Ibid., Vol. 1:334
23. Ibid., Vol. 1:334
24. Ibid., Vol. 1:334
25. Ibid., Vol. 1:334
26. Ibid., Vol. 1:334-335
27. Ibid., Vol. 1:336
28. Ibid., Vol. 1:336
29. Ibid., Vol. 1:337
30. Ibid., Vol. 1:337-338

31 Ibid., Vol. 1:338
32 IBID., Vol. 1:338
33 Ibid., Vol. 1:338-339
34 Ibid., Vol. 1:339
35 Ibid., Vol. 1:339
36 Ibid., Vol. 1:339-340
37 Ibid., Vol. 1:340
38 Ibid., Vol. 1:342
39 Ibid., Vol. 1:342
40 Melvoin, Richard I. *New England Outpost: War and Society in Colonial Deerfield.* New York: W. W. Norton & Company, 1989, 243
41 Ibid., 243

THE CLOSE OF QUEEN ANNE'S WAR

1 Sheldon, George. *A History of Deerfield Massachusetts: The Times When and The People by Whom It Was Settled, Unsettled and Resettled.* Deerfield, Mass: Pocumtuck Valley Memorial Association, Reprint 2004, Vol. 1:322-323
2 Ibid., Vol. 1:358
3 Ibid., Vol. 1:359
4 Ibid., Vol. 1:359-360
5 Ibid., Vol. 1:360
6 Ibid., Vol. 1:360
7 Ibid., Vol. 1:360
8 Ibid., Vol. 1:361
9 Ibid., Vol. 1:361
10 Ibid., Vol. 1:361
11 Ibid., Vol. 1:361
12 Ibid., Vol. 1:361-362
13 Ibid., Vol. 1:363
14 Ibid., Vol. 1:363
15 Vol. 1:363-364
16 Ibid., Vol. 1:364

17 Ibid., Vol. 1:364
18 Ibid., Vol. 1:364
19 Ibid., Vol. 1:364-365
20 Ibid., Vol. 1:365
21 Ibid., Vol. 1:365
22 Ibid., Vol. 1:365
23 Ibid., Vol. 1:366
24 Ibid., Vol. 1:366
25 Ibid., Vol. 1:366
26 Ibid., Vol. 1:366-367
27 Ibid., Vol. 1:367
28 Ibid., Vol. 1:373
29 Ibid., Vol. 1:373
30 Ibid., Vol. 1:373
31 Coleman, Emma L. *New England Captives Carried to Canada,* Westminster MD, Heritage Books, Reprint 2008, Vol. 2:81
32 Sheldon, George. *A History of Deerfield Massachusetts: The Times When and The People by Whom It Was Settled, Unsettled and Resettled.* Deerfield, Mass: Pocumtuck Valley Memorial Association, Reprint 2004, Vol. 1:373-374
33 Ibid., Vol. 1:375
34 Ibid., Vol. 1:375-376
35 Ibid., Vol. 1:376-377
36 Ibid., Vol. 1:377
37 Ibid., Vol. 1:377
38 Ibid., Vol. 1:378
39 Ibid., Vol. 1:378
40 Ibid., Vol. 1:379
41 Ibid., Vol. 1:379
42 Ibid., Vol. 1:381
43 Ibid., Vol. 1:381
44 Ibid., Vol. 1:382
45 Ibid., Vol. 1:383
46 Ibid., Vol. 1:383
47 Ibid., Vol. 1:383

48 Ibid., Vol. 1:384
49 Ibid., Vol. 1:384
50 Ibid., Vol. 1:384

THE AFTERMATH OF QUEEN ANNE'S WAR

1 Haefeli, Evan and Sweeney, Kevin. *Captors and Captives: The 1704 French And Indian Raid on Deerfield*. Amherst Mass: University of Massachusetts Press, 2003, 240
2 Ibid., 240-241
3 Ibid., 241
4 Ibid., 241
5 Ibid., 241-242
6 Ibid., 242
7 Sheldon, George. *A History of Deerfield Massachusetts: The Times When and The People by Whom It Was Settled, Unsettled and Resettled*. Deerfield, Mass: Pocumtuck Valley Memorial Association, Reprint 2004, Vol. 1:47
8 Ibid., Vol. 2:317
9 Baker, C. Alice. *True Stories of New England Captives Carried to Canada during the Old French and Indian Wars*. Westminster MD: Heritage Books Inc., Reprint 2007, 220
10 Ibid., 220
11 Haefeli, Evan and Sweeney, Kevin. *Captors and Captives: The 1704 French And Indian Raid on Deerfield*. Amherst Mass: University of Massachusetts Press, 2003, 285
12 Baker, C. Alice. *True Stories of New England Captives Carried to Canada during the Old French and Indian Wars*. Westminster MD: Heritage Books Inc., Reprint 2007, 221
13 Coleman, Emma L. *New England Captives Carried to Canada,* Westminster MD, Heritage Books, Reprint 2008, Vol. 2:119-120
14 Ibid., Vol. 2:119
15 Sheldon, George. *A History of Deerfield Massachusetts: The Times When and The People by Whom It Was Settled, Unsettled and Resettled*. Deerfield, Mass: Pocumtuck Valley Memorial Association, Reprint 2004, Vol.

1:343-344

16. Baker, C. Alice. *True Stories of New England Captives Carried to Canada during the Old French and Indian Wars.* Westminster MD: Heritage Books Inc., Reprint 2007, 220-221
17. Sheldon, George. *A History of Deerfield Massachusetts: The Times When and The People by Whom It Was Settled, Unsettled and Resettled.* Deerfield, Mass: Pocumtuck Valley Memorial Association, Reprint 2004, Vol. 1:346
18. Ibid., Vol. 1:346
19. Ibid., Vol. 1:346
20. Ibid., Vol. 1:346
21. Williams, John. *The Redeemed Captive Returning to Zion.* Bedford MA, Applewood Books, Reprint 1853
22. Coleman, Emma L. *New England Captives Carried to Canada,* Westminster MD, Heritage Books, Reprint 2008, Vol. 2:127
23. Baker, C. Alice. *True Stories of New England Captives Carried to Canada during the Old French and Indian Wars.* Westminster MD: Heritage Books Inc., Reprint 2007, 221
24. Coleman, Emma L. *New England Captives Carried to Canada,* Westminster MD, Heritage Books, Reprint 2008, Vol. 2:127
25. Ibid., Vol. 2:127
26. Ibid., Vol. 2:128
27. Ibid., Vol. 2:127
28. Ibid., Vol. 2:127
29. Sheldon, George. *A History of Deerfield Massachusetts: The Times When and The People by Whom It Was Settled, Unsettled and Resettled.* Deerfield, Mass: Pocumtuck Valley Memorial Association, Reprint 2004, Vol. 1:343
30. Coleman, Emma L. *New England Captives Carried to Canada,* Westminster MD, Heritage Books, Reprint 2008, Vol. 2:118-119
31. Ibid., Vol. 2:119
32. Ibid., Vol. 2:120
33. Ibid., Vol. 2:120
34. Ibid., Vol. 2:120-121
35. Ibid., Vol. 2:120-121
36. Ibid., Vol. 2:124
37. Ibid., Vol. 2:125

38   Ibid., Vol. 2:125
39   Ibid., Vol. 2:125
40   Ibid., Vol. 2:125
41   Ibid., Vol. 2:126
42   Ibid., Vol. 2:126
43   Sheldon, George. *A History of Deerfield Massachusetts: The Times When and The People by Whom It Was Settled, Unsettled and Resettled.* Deerfield, Mass: Pocumtuck Valley Memorial Association, Reprint 2004, Vol. 1:347-348

SUBSEQUENT DEERFIELD WARS

1   *French and Indian War.* Wikipedia. http://en.wikipedia.org/wiki/French_and_Indian_War
2   Historic Deerfield, Inc. *A Brief History of Deerfield Massachusetts.* Old Deerfield, Mass: 1972

APPENDIX C

1   Greenlee, Ralph Stebbins and Greenlee, Robert Lemuel. *The Stebbins Genealogy, Volumes 1&2.* Chicago Illinois, Printed Privately, 1904 (reprinted on CD), 51
2   Ibid., 74-75
3   Stebbins Ancestral Society. Cousins CD. Family Tree Maker
4   Greenlee, Ralph Stebbins and Greenlee, Robert Lemuel. The Stebbins Genealogy, Volumes 1&2. Chicago Illinois, Printed Privately, 1904 (reprinted on CD), 103
5   Greenlee, Ralph Stebbins and Greenlee, Robert Lemuel. The Stebbins Genealogy, Volumes 1&2. Chicago Illinois, Printed Privately, 1904 (reprinted on CD), 108
6   Ibid., 163
7   Robinson, Ivan N. Interview. French Genealogical Society, Tolland CT (Sources Drouin & Tanguay)
8   Greenlee, Ralph Stebbins and Greenlee, Robert Lemuel. The Stebbins

Genealogy, Volumes 1&2. Chicago Illinois, Printed Privately, 1904 (reprinted on CD), 1032

9   Stebbins Ancestral Society. Cousins CD. Family Tree Maker
10   Coleman, Emma L. New England Captives Carried to Canada. Westminster MD, Heritage Books, Reprint 2008, 127
11   Stebbins Ancestral Society. Cousins CD. Family Tree Maker
12   Coleman, Emma L. New England Captives Carried to Canada. Westminster MD, Heritage Books, Reprint 2008, 127
13   Stebbins Ancestral Society. Cousins CD. Family Tree Maker
14   Coleman, Emma L. New England Captives Carried to Canada. Westminster MD, Heritage Books, Reprint 2008, 127
15   Robinson, Ivan N. Interview. French Genealogical Society, Tolland CT (Sources Drouin & Tanguay)
16   Stebbins Ancestral Society. Cousins CD. Family Tree Maker
17   Robinson, Ivan N. Interview. French Genealogical Society, Tolland CT (Sources Drouin & Tanguay)
18   Stebbins Ancestral Society. Cousins CD. Family Tree Maker
19   Coleman, Emma L. New England Captives Carried to Canada. Westminster MD, Heritage Books, Reprint 2008, 127
20   Robinson, Ivan N. Interview. French Genealogical Society, Tolland CT (Sources Drouin & Tanguay)
21   Coleman, Emma L. New England Captives Carried to Canada. Westminster MD, Heritage Books, Reprint 2008, 127
22   Stebbins Ancestral Society. Cousins CD. Family Tree Maker
23   Coleman, Emma L. New England Captives Carried to Canada. Westminster MD, Heritage Books, Reprint 2008, 127
24   Stebbins Ancestral Society. Cousins CD. Family Tree Maker
25   Coleman, Emma L. New England Captives Carried to Canada. Westminster MD, Heritage Books, Reprint 2008, 127
26   Robinson, Ivan N. Interview. French Genealogical Society, Tolland CT (Sources Drouin & Tanguay)
27   Stebbins Ancestral Society. Cousins CD. Family Tree Maker
28   Greenlee, Ralph Stebbins and Greenlee, Robert Lemuel. The Stebbins Genealogy, Volumes 1&2. Chicago Illinois, Printed Privately, 1904 (reprinted on CD), 159

29 Ibid., 160-161
30 Ibid., 1032
31 Ibid., 1032
32 Robinson, Ivan N. Interview. French Genealogical Society, Tolland CT (Sources Drouin & Tanguay)
33 Stebbins Ancestral Society. Cousins CD. Family Tree Maker
34 Greenlee, Ralph Stebbins and Greenlee, Robert Lemuel. The Stebbins Genealogy, Volumes 1&2. Chicago Illinois, Printed Privately, 1904 (reprinted on CD), 1036-1037
35 Robinson, Ivan N. Interview. French Genealogical Society, Tolland CT (Sources Drouin & Tanguay)
36 Stebbins Ancestral Society. Cousins CD. Family Tree Maker
37 Robinson, Ivan N. Interview. French Genealogical Society, Tolland CT (Sources Drouin & Tanguay)
38 Greenlee, Ralph Stebbins and Greenlee, Robert Lemuel. The Stebbins Genealogy, Volumes 1&2. Chicago Illinois, Printed Privately, 1904 (reprinted on CD), 1037
39 Greenlee, Ralph Stebbins and Greenlee, Robert Lemuel. The Stebbins Genealogy, Volumes 1&2. Chicago Illinois, Printed Privately, 1904 (reprinted on CD), 1037
40 Stebbins, H.R., Stebbins Family Tree, Ancestry.com
41 Ibid.
42 Ibid.
43 Ibid
44 Ibid.

BIBLIOGRAPHY

Baker, C. Alice. *True Stories of New England Captives Carried to Canada during the Old French and Indian Wars.* Westminster MD: Heritage Books Inc., Reprint 2007

Bancroft, George. *History of the United States: from the Discovery of the American Continent* (2 vols.). Boston: Little Brown, 1837

Bourne, Russell. *The Red Kings Rebellion: Racial Politics in New England 1675-1678.* Atheneum, Macmillan Publishing Company, 1990

Calloway, Colin G. *After King Phillip's War: Presence and Persistence in Indian New England.* Hanover NH: Dartmouth College, University Press of New England, 1977

Calloway, Colin G. *The Western Abenakis of Vermont, 1600-1800.* University of Oklahoma Press, Norman Publishing Division of the University, 1994

Coleman, Emma L. *New England Captives Carried to Canada.* Westminster MD, Heritage Books, Reprint 2008

Cronon, William. *Changes in the Land: Indians Colonists, and the Ecology of New England.* New York: Hill and Wang, 1983

Drake, Samuel A. *The Border Wars of New England.* Williamstown MA, Corner House Publishers, 1973

Flynt, Suzanne. "The Old Indian House Door." *Historic Deerfield* Spring 2004 Volume 4 Number 1: 17-20

French and Indian War. Wikipedia. http://en.wikipedia.org/wiki/French_and_Indian_War

Greenlee, Ralph Stebbins and Greenlee, Robert Lemuel. *The Stebbins Genealogy, Volumes 1&2*. Chicago Illinois, Printed Privately, 1904 (reprinted on CD)

Haefeli, Evan and Sweeney, Kevin. *Captors and Captives: The 1704 French And Indian Raid on Deerfield*. Amherst Mass: University of Massachusetts Press, 2003

Historic Deerfield, Inc. *A Brief History of Deerfield Massachusetts*. Old Deerfield, Mass: 1972

Hubbard, William. *The History of the Indian Wars in New England from the First Settlement to the Termination of the War with King Philip*. Samuel G. Drake (ed.). New York: Lenox Hill, 1971 (reprint)

Jennings, Francis. *The Invasion of America: Indians, Colonialism, and the Cant of Conquest*. Chapel Hill: University of North Carolina Press, 1975

King Williams War. Wikipedia Http://en.wikipedia.org/wiki/King_William%27s_War

Main Memory Network. *Death of Father Sebastian Rale* http://www.mainememory.net/artifact/7530/enlarge

McDonald, Heather. *Interview.* St. Regis Mohawk Reservation. 2012

Melvoin, Richard I. *New England Outpost: War and Society in Colonial Deerfield*. New York: W. W. Norton & Company, 1989

Moogk, Peter N. *La Nouvelle France: The Making of French Canada - a Cultural History*. East Lansing, MI: Michigan State University Press, *2002*

Penhallow, Samuel. *History of the Indian Wars.* Williamstown MA, Corner House Publishers, 1973 reprint

Robinson, Ivan N. *Interview.* French Genealogical Society, Tolland CT (Sources Drouin & Tanguay)

Sheldon, George. *A History of Deerfield Massachusetts: The Times When and The People by Whom It Was Settled, Unsettled and Resettled Vols. 1&2* Deerfield, Mass: Pocumtuck Valley Memorial Association, Reprint 2004

Stebbins Ancestral Society. Cousins CD. Family Tree Maker

Stebbins, H.R., *Stebbins Family Tree,* Ancestry.com

Sweeney, Kevin. "*Rediscovering 1704.* Historic Deerfield Spring 2004 Volume 4 Number 1: 2-7

Tougias, Michael. "King Philip's War in New England, (America's First Major Indian War)" *The History Place.* 1997: 10 Sept.2000<http://www.historyplace.com/specials/ calendar/docs-pix/aug-kingphilip.htm>

Williams, John. *The Redeemed Captive Returning to Zion.* Bedford MA, Applewood Books, Reprint 1853

Williams, Stephen W. An Appendix and Notes. 137-192 (see Williams, John)

Williams Captives Redeemed *King Williams War.* Wikipedia

INDEX

A
Adams, James 128, 131
Alexander, Dorothy 48, 153 [see also Dorothy Stebbins]
Alexander, John 48, 153
Alexander, Joseph 110, 149
Alexander, Robert 48
Allen, Edward 120, 134
Allen, John 120
Allen, Sarah 120, 149
Allison, John 91
Allison, Thomas 91
Allyn, Edward 54
Amrusus 161
Anawan 136
Andrews, Samuel 148
Andros, Sir Edmund 50
Appleton, Capt. Samuel 133, 134
Ardaway, Johannah 139
Armes, William 55
Arms, John 116, 144, 149
Ashpelon 49
Atkinson, Hannah 143
Avery, John 143

B
Barber, Josiah 142
Bartlett, Abijah 142
Bartlett, Robert 20
Barrett, Benjamin 48, 54, 148
Bartlett, Samue 46, 121
Battis, Thomas 123
Beaubasin 128

Beaman, Simon 54, 149
Beers, Captain 32
Beers, Ephraim 48
Belcher, Gov. Jonathan 166
Belding, Daniel 55, 69
Belding, Nathaniel 55, 92
Bennett, James 20
Benton 124
Bodman, Joseph 48
Boltwood, Sgt. 115
Borland, John 129
Bradley, Hannah 131
Bradley, Joseph 130
Bridgeman, John 110
Bonner, Captain 131
Bouat, Demoiselle Marguerite 158
Boucher, Ensign Rene 80, 91, 99
Bridgeman, John 98, 117
Brooks, Ebenezer 48, 92, 96
Brooks, Nathaniel 48, 134, 135, 149
Broughton, Mary 42
Broughton, Thomas 48
Brown, James 48
Burt, Benjamin 131, 149
Burt, Christopher 131
Burt, John 131, 149
Burt, Sarah 131, 149
Burt, Seaborne 131

C
Carter, John 149, 157
Carter, Marah 110, 149
Carter, Samuel 89, 149

Catlin, John 91, 104, 149
Catlin, John Sr. 54, 55, 59
Catlin, Joseph 94, 96, 115
Catlin, Mr. 49
Catlin, Mrs. 106
Chauk 31
Choate, Benjamin 124, 125
Church, Benjamin 40, 48, 94, 117
Church, Jonathon 48
Church, Samuel 116
Clary, John 143
Cleeson, Joseph 57, 116, 149
Cornbury, Governor 68, 130, 135
Courtemanche, Captain 128, 129
Crocker, Lieut. William 146
Crossman, Dr. 123

D
D' Anjou 60
de Batilly, Ensign Francois-Marie Margane 94, 99
de Beaucours, Captain 122, 123
de Beaulac, Claude Hertel 152
de Beauville, Captain 128
de Chambly, Captain 135
de Dupuis, Sieur 143
de Joncaire, Sieur 142
de Iberville, Pierre Le Moyne 111
de LaPeriere 143
de Montcalm, Marquis 111
de Montigny, Sieur 121, 122
de Niverville, Jean Baptiste Boucher 152
de Noyon, Aaron 151, 154, 155
de Noyon, Marguerite [see Abigail Stebbins]
de Noyon [Desnoions], Jacques 80-92, 91, 111, 114, 151-155, 159, 160
de Ramezay, Gov. Claude 100, 143

de Rouville, Lieut. Jean Baptiste Hertel 64, 65, 80, 84-88, 94, 96, 99, 100, 109-111, 120, 141, 143
de Tonty, Alphonse 152, 158
de Vaudreuil, Gov. Phillipe de Rigand 64, 100, 121-130, 134, 135, 137, 140-148
de Vercheres, Sieur 144
Drummer, Lieut. Gov. William 164
Dudley, Governor Joseph 50, 65, 66, 69, 71, 76, 126-131, 134, 135, 137, 140-146
Dudley, William 129
Dulhut, Daniel Greysolon 80
Dutch, Robert 36

E
Eastman, Joseph 89, 149
Edgerly, Joseph 132
Eliot, John 38
Evans, John 59

F
Field, Ebenezer 142
Field, John 91, 149
Field, Samuel 47
Fisher, Left 17
Frank [slave] 50, 89, 110, 149
Frary, Samson 91
French, Abigail 143, 149
French, Freedom 143, 149
French, Mary 143, 146
French, Martha 143, 149
French, Thomas [son of Thomas] 143, 149
French, Corp. Thomas 50, 55, 120, 131, 143, 149

G
Gillette, Joseph 48

Goselin, Louis 81
Granger, Robert 143
Graylock 146
Green, John 142

H
Hastings, Benjamin 48, 50
Hastings, Samuel 48, 149
Hastings, Thomas 49
Hawks, John Sr. 91
Hawks, Sgt. John 57, 61, 67, 123
Hawley, Joseph 46
Hertel, Francois 84, 152
Hickson, Jacob 121, 149
Hill, Samuel 128, 129, 133
Hinsdale, Mary 131, 149
Hinsdale, Samuel 83
Holyoke, Captain 40
Hoyt [Hoite], Lieut. David 47, 54, 61, 67, 69, 78, 94, 96, 115
Hoyt, David Sr. 89, 121, 149
Hoyt, Deacon 49, 54, 125
Hoyt, Jonathan 129, 149
Hoyt, Mary 95
How, Capt. 147
Hubbard, Barijah 36, 140
Huggins, Margaret 121
Hurst, Thomas 48, 149
Hutchinson, Moses 121
Hutchinson, Ralph 20

J
James, Ebenezer 121
James, Hannah 121
James, Miriam 121
James, Nathan 121
James, Obadiah 121
James, Samuel 121

James, Sarah [wife] 121
James, Sarah 121
James [Gems-Sansoucy], Marguerite 152
Jennings, Benjamin 142
Jennings, Joseph 142
Jones, Benoni 121
Jones, Ebenezer 121
Jones, Esther 121
Jones, Jonathan 121
Juauguelatt 19

K
Kellogg, Martin 142, 149
Kellogg, Sarah 92
King Charles II 59, 60
King James II 50, 53, 60
King Louis XIV 57, 60
King Philip 24-26, 34, 40
King William III 53, 60

L
Lathrop [Lothrope], Captain Thomas 24, 32-38
Legrain [Lavalle], Charles 152
Legardeur, Charles 99, 100
Littlefield, Josiah 144
Livingstone, Capt. John 126
Lyman, Caleb 121

M
Manreuil, Father 144
Marchant, Lewis 140
Marsh, John 97, 98, 149
Massasoit 24
Mather, Samuel 31, 34
Matoonas 34
Mattamuck 34
Mattoon, Philip 42, 91, 149

Menard, Jean Baptiste 156
Menard, Marguerite 152, 156
Meriel, Father 156
Metacom 24, 26
Milewski, Kazimierz A. 23
Moseley [Mosely], Captain Samuel 33, 36 – 39, 153
Munn, Benjamin 92
Munn, Sylvia 103
Muttawmp 36

N
Newberry, Capt. Benjamin 119
Newgate, Peter 123
Nicholson, Gen. 142-145
Nims, Godfrey 20, 48, 78, 91
Nims, John 68, 86
Northam, Samuel 54

O
Olmstead, William 124
One-Eyed John 55
Onequelat 21

P
Parsons, Aaron 140
Parsons, Capt. John 140
Parsons, Joseph 48, 150
Parsons, Samuel 140
Parthenia 50, 89
Partridge, Col. Samuel 69, 77-79, 98, 119, 124, 126, 131, 134, 138, 141-147
Passaconaway 26
Penchason 34
Phelps, Mary 56
Pitt, William 166
Plympton, John Sgt. 42, 43
Ponchartrain 140

Porter, Aaron 143
Price, Elizabeth 82, 83, 149
Price, Robert 91
Pumry [Pomroy], Joshua 50, 149
Pynchon, John 17-20, 30-33 ,42, 66, 78

Q
Queen Anne 59, 60
Queen Mary 53

R
Rasle, Father 163, 164
Rice, Deacon Edmund 134
Richards, John 66, 91, 92
Robert, Tigo 50
Root, John 42, 48
Russell, Thomas 123

S
Sagamore, Sam 34
Salisbury, Capt. 42
Sanford, William 148, 149
Sangumachu 34
Sansoucy, Marguerite 136
Searls, Ebenezer 116
Searls, Elisha 121
Searles, John 121
Seger, Henry 135
Sergeant, John 166
Sheldon, Deacon 49, 123, 130, 135
Sheldon, Hannah [John Sr's wife] 93
Sheldon, Hannah [Chapin] 47, 92, 93, 128
Sheldon, Sgt. John 47, 50, 54
Sheldon, John Junior 94
Sheldon, Mary 128, 131
Sheldon, Mercy 94, 105
Sheldon [Shelton], Ensign 48, 54, 61, 65, 67, 69, 92, 105, 125-134, 141, 146

Shute, Governor 164
Schuyler, Maj./Col. Peter 68, 134, 135, 138-143, 146, 148
Smead, John 96, 99, 116
Smead, Samuel l91
Smead, William 50
Smith, Martin 48, 55, 56, 91
Smith, Phillip 56
Smith, Preserved 124
Smith, Sarah 56, 57
Staats, Lieut. 149
Stebbins, Abigail [De Noyon, Marguerite] 82, 114, 118, 149-158
Stebbins, Benjamin 96
Stebbins, Dorothy 82, 118, 142 [see also Dorothy Alexander]
Stebbins, Ebenezer [Benoni's son] 48, 51, 56
Stebbins, Ebenezer [John's son] [Jacques Charles Stebbens] 82, 114, 151, 154, 157
Stebbins, John Sr. 17
Stebbins, John III 82, 118, 154
Stebbins, Joseph 82, 118, 151, 154, 156
Stebbins, Rowland 17, 18
Stebbins, Samuel 82, 118, 151, 154
Stebbins, Thankful [John's dau.] [Louise Therese Steben] 82, 114, 118, 152, 154, 160, 161
Stebbbins, Thankful [Benoni's dau.] 48
Stevens, Andrew 82, 83, 92
Stevens, Elizabeth [Price] 82, 83
Stockwell, Quintin 42, 43
Stoddard, Lieut. John 89, 139, 147
Stoddard, Reverend Solomon 73, 76, 78
Strong, Jedediah 56
Strong, Samuel 145
Strong, Samuel [son] 145

T
Tatason 34
Taylor, James 130
Taylor, Capt. John 120, 121
Taylor, Sgt. Samuel 148
Theodota, Heborah 84
Treat, Robert 32
Tigo [Santiago], Roberto 50
Turner, Captain 40

V
Vetch, Capt. 128-130

W
Waite, Sgt. 115
Walcott, John 142
Warner, Ebenezer 116, 149
Washington, George 165
Wattanummon 89
Watts, Captain 32
Webb, Patience 121
Webb, Patience [dau.] 121
Wells, John 130, 139
Wells, Capt. Jonathan 48, 49, 54, 61, 66-69, 78, 85, 93, 96, 116, 124, 126
Wells, Lincoln 105
Wells, Lieut. Thomas 51, 53, 116, 124
White, Henry 54, 56
Whiting, Col. William 122, 140
William of Orange 59
Williams, Esther 89, 128, 134, 149
Williams, Eunice 89, 149, 161
Williams, Mrs. Eunice 89, 112, 149
Williams, Jerusha 89
Williams, John [John's son] 89
Williams, Reverend John 49, 50, 57, 61, 62, 67, 69, 73, 85, 88, 89, 94, 95, 97, 107, 123, 127-138, 143-145, 149, 162

213

Williams, Roger 26
Williams, Samuel 129, 146, 149
Williams, Stephen 89, 110, 120, 121, 129, 136, 142, 148, 149
Williams, Warham 89, 134, 149
Williams, Zebediah 68, 86, 132
Willard, Samuel 131
Winslow, Major Josiah 26
Winthrop, Gov. Fitz-John 68, 79, 98, 118, 157
Wright, Lieut. Abel 140
Wright, Capt. Benjamin 140, 147
Wright, Hannah 140
Wright, Henry 140
Wright, Martha 140

Y
York, Samuel 83

AUTHOR'S BIOGRAPHY

Currently genealogy is his primary hobby. He is a member of the Stebbins Ancestral Society, the RI Ancestral Society and has DNA-linked family trees on Ancestry.com. Being a visual person, he created a superior way of presenting a family's pedigree in a compact, color-coded manner [see Appendix A & B, printed in B&W by necessity].

A graduate of Michigan State University with a BS in Natural Science in 1966, Mr. Stebbins started teaching Chemistry and Physics in a Connecticut high school. He worked part-time as a roofer, wedding photographer and gymnastics coach.

An avid sailor, he raced various sailboats with a local club. As a sailboat cruiser, he sailed in southern New England waters, and ultimately made two dream trips to sail near Bora Bora and among other nearby islands. He, and his wife Dianne, enjoy traveling on cruise ships to other distant shores.

Made in the USA
Middletown, DE
03 October 2022